Norwegian Life
An Account Of Past And Contemporary Conditions And Progress In Norway And Sweden

by

Ed. Ethlyn T. Clough

Norwegian Life
An Account Of Past And Contemporary Conditions And Progress In Norway And Sweden
by Ed. Ethlyn T. Clough

ISBN: 978-93-64288-27-9

Published by

DOUBLE 9 BOOKS

2/13-B, Ansari Road
Daryaganj, New Delhi – 110002
info@double9books.com
www.double9books.com
Tel. 011-40042856

ABOUT THE EDITOR

Ethlyn T. Clough was an American writer and scholar known for her deep interest in Scandinavian culture and literature, particularly focusing on Norway. Born in the late 19th century, Clough dedicated much of her life to studying and writing about Norwegian society, history, and literature. Clough's fascination with Norway stemmed from her travels and studies, which allowed her to immerse herself in the country's rich cultural heritage. She became a respected authority on Norwegian life, contributing valuable insights through her writings that spanned both academic works and popular literature. Her notable work, "Norwegian Life: An Account of Past and Contemporary," stands as a testament to her scholarly approach and dedication to presenting a comprehensive view of Norwegian society. In this book, Clough not only explored historical aspects but also delved into contemporary issues, offering readers a thorough understanding of Norway's cultural evolution and societal dynamics. Ethlyn T. Clough's writings often reflected her admiration for Norway's natural beauty, its literary achievements, and its progressive social policies. Her work contributed significantly to promoting cultural exchange and understanding between Norway and the United States, where she shared her insights and findings with audience eager to learn about Scandinavian culture. While specific biographical details about Ethlyn T. Clough are sparse, her legacy lives on through her writings, which continue to be valued for their scholarly rigor, cultural sensitivity, and profound appreciation for the complexities of Norwegian life.

CONTENTS

PREFACE

An excursion into Norwegian life has for the student all the charm of the traveler's real journey through the pleasant valleys of the Norse lands. Much of this charm is explained by the tenacity of the people to the homely virtues of honesty and thrift, to their customs which testify to their home-loving character, and to their quaint costumes. It is a genuine delight to study and visit these lands, because they are the least, perhaps in Europe, affected by the leveling hand of cosmopolitan ideas. Go where you will,—to England, about Germany, down into Italy,—everywhere, the same monotonous sameness is growing more oppressive every year. But in Norway and Sweden there is still an originality, a type, if you please, that has resisted the growth of an artificial life, and gives to students a charm which is even more alluring than modern cities with their treasures and associations.

The student takes up Norwegian life as one of the subjects which has been comparatively little explored, and is, therefore replete with freshness and delight. This little book can not by any means more than lift the curtain to view the fields of historical and literary interest and the wondrous life lived in the deep fiords of Viking land. But its brief pages will have, at least, the merit of giving information on a subject about which only too little has been written. Taken in all, there are scarcely half a dozen recent books circulating in American literary channels on these interesting lands, and for one reason or another, most of these are unsuited for club people. There is an urgent call for a comprehensive book which will waste no time in non-essentials,—a book that can be read in a few sittings and yet will give a glimpse over this quaint and wondrously interesting corner of Europe. This book has been prepared, as have all the predecessors in this series, by the help of many who have written most delightfully of striking things in Norwegian life. One has specialized in one thing, while another has been allured by another subject. Accordingly, "Norwegian Life" is the product of many, each inspired with feeling and admiration for the one or two subjects on which he has written better than on any others. Liberty has been taken to make a few verbal changes in order to give to the story the unity and smoothness desired, and a key-letter at the end of each chapter refers the reader to a page at the close where due credits are given.

J.M. HALL.

CHAPTER I
PREHISTORIC AND EARLY HISTORIC TIMES

A glance at the map will show that the Scandinavian Peninsula, that immense stretch of land running from the Arctic Ocean to the North Sea, and from the Baltic to the Atlantic, covering an area of nearly three hundred thousand square miles, is, next to Russia, the largest territorial division of Europe. Surrounded by sea on all sides but one, which gives it an unparalleled seaboard of over two thousand miles, it hangs on the continent by its frontier line with Russia in Lapland. Down the middle of this seabound continent, dividing it into two nearly equal parts, runs a chain of mountains not inappropriately called Kölen, or Keel. The name suggests the image which the aspect of the land calls to mind, that of a huge ship floating keel upwards on the face of the ocean. This keel forms the frontier line between the kingdoms of Norway and Sweden: Sweden to the east, sloping gently from the hills to the Baltic, Norway to the west, running more abruptly down from their watershed to the Atlantic.

Norway (in the old Norse language *Noregr*, or *Nord-vegr, i.e.*, the North Way), according to archaeological explorations, appears to have been inhabited long before historical time. The antiquarians maintain that three populations have inhabited the North: a Mongolian race and a Celtic race, types of which are to be found in the Finns and the Laplanders in the far North, and, finally, a Caucasian race, which immigrated from the South and drove out the Celtic and Laplandic races, and from which the present inhabitants are descended. The Norwegians, or Northmen (Norsemen), belong to a North-Germanic branch of the Indo-European race; their nearest kindred are the Swedes, the Danes, and the Goths. The original home of the race is supposed to have been the mountain region of Balkh, in Western Asia, whence from time to time families and tribes migrated in different directions. It is not known when the ancestors of the Scandinavian peoples left the original home in Asia; but it is probable that their earliest settlements in Norway were made in the second century before the Christian era.

The Scandinavian peoples, although comprising the oldest and most unmixed race in Europe, did not realize until very late the value of writing chronicles or reviews of historic events. Thus the names of heroes and kings of the remotest past are helplessly forgotten, save as they come to us in legend and folk-song, much of which we must conclude is imaginary, beautiful as it is. But Mother Earth has revealed to us, at the spade of the archaeologist, trustworthy and irrefutable accounts of the age and the various degrees of civilization of the race which inhabited the Scandinavian Peninsula in prehistoric times. Splendid specimens now extant in numerous museums prove that Scandinavia, like most other countries, has had a Stone Age, a Bronze Age, and an Iron Age, and that each of these periods reached a much higher development than in other countries.

The Scandinavian countries are for the first time mentioned by the historians of antiquity in an account of a journey which Pyteas from Massilia (the present Marseille) made throughout Northern Europe, about 300 B.C. He visited Britain, and there heard of a great country, Thule, situated six days' journey to the north, and verging on the Arctic Sea. The inhabitants in Thule were an agricultural people who gathered their harvest into big houses for threshing, on account of the very few sunny days and the plentiful rain in their regions. From corn and honey they prepared a beverage (probably mead).

Pliny the Elder, who himself visited the shores of the Baltic in the first century after Christ, is the first to mention plainly the name of Scandinavia. He says that he has received advices of immense islands "recently discovered from Germany." The most famous of these islands was Scandinavia, of as yet unexplored size; the known parts were inhabited by a people called *hilleviones*, who gave it the name of another world. He mentions Scandia, Nerigon, the largest of them all, and Thule. Scandia and Scandinavia are only different forms of the same name, denoting the southernmost part of the peninsula, and still preserved in the name of the province of Scania in Sweden. Nerigon stands for Norway, the northern part of which is mentioned as an island by the name of Thule. The classical writers were ignorant of the fact that Scandinavia was one great peninsula, because the northern parts were as yet uninhabited and their physical connection with Finland and Russia unknown. That the Romans were later acquainted with the Scandinavian countries is evidenced from the fact that great numbers of Roman coins have been found in excavating, also vessels of bronze and glass, weapons, etc., as well as works of art, all turned out of the workshops in Rome or its provinces. There, no doubt, existed a regular traffic over the Baltic, through Germany, between the Scandinavian countries and the Roman provinces.

The first settlers probably knew little of agriculture, but made their living by fishing and hunting. In time, however, they commenced to clear away the timber that covered the land in the valleys and on the sides of the mountains and to till the ground. At the earliest times of which the historical tales or *Sagas* tell us anything with regard to the social conditions, the land was divided among the free peasant-proprietors, or *bonde class*. Bonde, in English translation, is usually called peasant; but this is not an equivalent; for with the word "peasant" we associate the idea of inferior social condition to the landed aristocracy of the country, while these peasants or bondes were themselves the highest class in the country. The land owned by a peasant was called his *udal*. By udal-right the land was kept in the family, and it could not be alienated or forfeited from the kindred who were udal-born to it. The free peasants might own many thralls or slaves, who were unfree men. These were mostly prisoners captured by the vikings on their expeditions to foreign shores; the owner could trade them away, or sell them, or even kill them without paying any fine or *man-bote* to the king, as in the case of killing a free man. As a rule, however, the slaves were not badly treated, and they were sometimes made free and given the right to acquire land.

In early days Norway consisted of a great number of small states called *Fylkis*, each a little kingdom by itself. The free peasants in a Fylki held general assemblies called *Things*, where laws were made and justice administered. No public acts were undertaken without the deliberation of a *Thing*. The *Thing* was sacred, and a breach of peace at the *thing-place* was considered a great crime. At the *Thing* there was also a hallowed place for the judges, or "lag-men," who expounded and administered the laws made by the *Thing*. Almost every crime could be expiated by the payment of fines, even if the accused had killed a person. But if a man killed another secretly, he was declared an assassin and an outlaw, was deprived of all his property, and could be killed by any one who wished to do so. The fine or man-bote was heavier, the higher the rank of the person killed.

The *Thing* or *Fylkis Thing* was not made up of representatives elected by the people, but was rather a primary assembly of the free udal-born peasant-proprietors of the district. There were leading men in the *fylki*, and each *fylki* had one or more chiefs, but they had to plead at the *Thing* like other free men. When there were several chiefs, they usually had the title of *herse*; but when the free men had agreed upon one chief, he was called *jarl* (earl), or king. The king was the commander in war, and usually performed the judicial functions; but he supported himself upon his own estates, and the free peasants paid no tax. The dignity of the king was usually inherited by his son, but if the heir was not to the liking of the people, they chose another. No man, however clear his right of succession, would think of assuming the title or power of a king except by the vote of the *Thing*. There he was presented to the people by a free peasant, and his right must be confirmed by the *Thing* before he could exert any act of kingly power. The king had a number of free men in his service, who had sworn allegiance to him in war and in peace. They were armed men, kept in pay, and were called *hird-men* or court-men, because they were members of the king's hird or court. If they were brave and faithful, they were often given high positions of trust; some were made *lendermen* (liegemen), or managers of the king's estates.

It is but natural that the ancient Norwegians should become warlike and brave men, since their firm religious belief was that those who died of sickness or old age would sink down into the dark abode of Hel (Helheim), and that only the brave men who fell in battle would be invited to the feasts in Odin's Hall. Sometimes the earls or kings would make war on their neighbors, either for conquest or revenge. But the time came when the countries of the north, with their poorly developed resources, became overpopulated, and the warriors had to seek other fields abroad. The viking cruises commenced, and for a long time the Norwegians continued to harry the coasts of Europe.

At first the viking expeditions were nothing but piracy, carried on for a livelihood. The name Viking is supposed to be derived from the word *vik*, a cove or inlet on the coast, in which they would harbor their ships and lie in wait for merchants sailing by. Soon these expeditions assumed a wider range and a wilder character, and historians of the time paint the horrors spread by the vikings in dark colors. In the English churches they had a day of prayer each week to invoke the aid of heaven against the harrying Northmen. In France the following formula was inserted in the church prayer: *"A furore Normannorum libera nos, o Domine!"* (Free us, O Lord, from the fury of the Northmen!)

Gradually the viking life assumed a nobler form. There appear to have been three stages or periods in the viking age. In the first one the vikings make casual visits with single ships to the shores of England, Ireland, France or Flanders, and when they have plundered a town or a convent, they return to their ships and sail away. In the second period their cruises assume a more regular character, and indicate some definite plan, as they take possession of certain points, where they winter, and from where they command the surrounding country. During the third period they no longer confine themselves to seeking booty, but act as real conquerors, take possession of the conquered territory, and rule it. As to the influence of the Northmen on the development of the countries visited in this last period, the eminent English writer, Samuel Laing, the translator of the *Heimskringla,* or the Sagas of the Norse kings, says:

"All that men hope for of good government and future improvement in their physical and moral condition—all that civilized men enjoy at this day of civil, religious, and political liberty—the British constitution, representative legislation, the trial by jury, security of property, freedom of mind and person, the influence of public opinion over the conduct of public affairs, the Reformation, the liberty of the press, the spirit of the age—all that is or has been of value to man in modern times as a member of society, either in Europe or in the New World, may be traced to the spark left burning upon our shores by these northern barbarians."

The authentic history begins with Halfdan the Swarthy, who reigned from the year 821 to 860. The Icelander Snorre Sturlason, who, in the twelfth century, wrote the *Heimskringla*, or Sagas of the Norse Kings, gives a long line of preceding kings of the Yngling race, the royal family to which Halfdan the Swarthy belonged; but that part of the Saga belongs to mythology rather than to history.

According to tradition, the Yngling family were descendants of Fiolner, the son of the god Frey. One of the surnames of the god was Yngve, from which the family derived the name Ynglings. King Halfdan was a wise man, a lover of truth and justice. He made good laws, which he observed himself and compelled others to observe. He fixed certain penalties for all crimes committed. His code of laws, called the Eidsiva Law, was adopted at a common *Thing* at Eidsvol, where about a thousand years later the present constitution of Norway was adopted.

One day in the spring of 860, when Halfdan the Swarthy was driving home from a feast across the Randsfjord, he broke through the ice and was drowned. He was so popular that, when his body was found, the leading men in each *Fylki* demanded to have him buried with them, believing that it would bring prosperity to the district. They at last agreed to divide the body into four parts, which were buried in four different districts. The trunk of the body was buried in a mound at Stien, Ringerike, where a little hill is still called Halfdan's Mound. And this Halfdan became the ancestor of the royal race of Norway.

Halfdan's son, Harald the Fairhaired, at the age of ten years succeeded his father on the throne of Norway, or it afterward proved to be the throne of United Norway. When he became old enough to marry, he sent his men to a girl named Gyda, a daughter of King Erik of Hordaland, who was brought up a foster-child in the house of a rich *Bonde* in Valders.

Harald had heard of her as a very beautiful though proud girl. When the men delivered their message, she answered that she would not marry a king who had no greater kingdom than a few *Fylkis* (districts), and she added that she thought it strange that "no king here in Norway will make the whole country subject to him, in the same way that Gorm the Old did in Denmark, or Erik at Upsala." When the messengers returned to the king, they advised him to punish her for her haughty words, but Harald said she had spoken well, and he made the solemn vow not to cut or comb his hair until he had subdued the whole of Norway, which he did, and became sole king of Norway. The decisive battle was a naval one in the Hafrsfjord, near the present city of Stavanger. After this battle, which occurred in 872, when he had been declared King of United Norway, he attended a feast, and the Earl of More cut his hair, which had not been cut or combed for ten years, and gave him the name of Fairhaired. Harald shortly afterward married Gyda.

From this time on, the history of Norway for nearly three hundred years consists mainly in internecine warfare among the various claimants of the throne, and the result of all this warfare was not only to exhaust the material resources of the people, but to drive a large proportion of the population to make viking excursions to win land elsewhere, and also to make peaceable settlements in other countries. Iceland was settled by the leading men of Norway in Harald the Fairhaired's reign because they would not submit to his rule and therefore emigrated to a land where they could rule. In 912 Duke Rollo with a large following conquered Normandy and settled there with many of his countrymen.

As the result of over three centuries of foreign and domestic war, Norway and her people and her industries were prostrate when in 1389 Queen Margaret of Denmark claimed the succession to the throne of Norway for her son Eric of Pomerania. The council of Norway and the people were willing to accept a union with a more populous country under a powerful sovereign in order to obtain peace and reestablish order and prosperity. Norway had not been conquered by Denmark, and the union was supposed to be equal. The Danish sovereigns, however, without directly interfering with the local laws and usages of the people of Norway, filled all the executive and administrative offices in Norway with Danes; the important commands in the army were also given exclusively to them. The result was that the interpretation and execution of the laws of the land were in the hands of foreigners, and Norway became and remained for four hundred years a province of Denmark and unable to throw off the yoke because her army was in the control and command of her oppressor, and her material resources inadequate to wage successful war against him.

Like Norway, the most that we know of prehistoric times in Sweden we gather from the early sagas, which are more or less faulty in their statements, romantic and tragic though they be. Like the Norwegians, the early Swedes are reported to have migrated from Asia under the leadership of a chief who called himself Odin. And for centuries under different kings and queens, the romantic and tragic story of Sweden goes on to form at last her authentic history. In this brief survey we can not go into details, and its history is very much the same as that of Norway, except that Sweden was oftener her own mistress and at longer intervals.

The sources of Swedish history during the first two centuries of the Middle Ages are very meager. This is a deplorable fact, for during that period Sweden passed through a great and thorough development, the various stages of which consequently are not easily traced. Before the year 1060, Sweden is an Old Teutonic state, certainly of later form and larger compass than the earliest of such, but with its democracy and its elective kingdom preserved. The older Sweden was, in regard to its constitution, a rudimentary union of states. The realm had come into existence through the cunning and violence of the king of the Sviar, who made way with the kings of the respective lands, making their communities pay homage to him. No change in the interior affairs of the different lands was thereby effected; they lost their outward political independence, but remained mutually on terms of perfect equality. They were united only through the king, who was the only center for the government of the union. No province had constitutionally more importance than the rest, no supremacy by one over the other existed. On this historic basis the Swedish realm was built, and rested firmly until the commencement of the Middle Ages. In the Old Swedish state-organism the various parts thus possessed a high degree of individualized and pulsating life; the empire as a whole was also powerful, although the royal dignity was its only institution. The king was the outward tie which bound the provinces together; besides him there was no power of state which embraced the whole realm. The affairs of state were decided upon by the king alone, as regard to war, or he had to gather the opinion of the Thing in each province, as any imperial representation did not exist and was entirely unknown, both in the modern sense and in the form of one provincial, or sectional, assembly deciding for all the others. In society there existed no classes. It was a democracy of free men, the slaves and free men enjoying no rights. The first centuries of the Middle Ages were one continued process of regeneration, the Swedish people being carried into the European circle of cultural development and made a communicant of Christianity. With the commencement of the thirteenth century, Sweden comes out of this process as a medieval state, in aspect entirely different to her past. The democratic equality among free men has turned into an aristocracy, with aristocratic institutions, the hereditary kingdom into an elective kingdom, while the provincial particularism and independence have given way to the constitution of a centralized, monopolistic state. No changes could be more fundamental.

The old provincial laws of Sweden are a great and important inheritance which this period has accumulated from heathen times. The laws were written down in the thirteenth and fourteenth centuries, but they bear every evidence of high antiquity. Many strophes are found in them of the same meter as those on the tombstones of the Viking Age and those in which the songs of the Edda are chiefly written. In other instances the texts consist of alliterative prose, which proves its earlier metrical form. The expressions have, in places, remained heathen, although used by Christians, who are ignorant of their true meaning, as, for instance, in the following formula of an oath, in the West Gothic law: *Sva se mer gud hull* (So help me the gods). In lieu of a missing literature of sagas and poetry, these provincial laws give a good insight into the character, morals, customs, and culture of the heathen and early Christian times of Sweden. From the point of philology they are also of great value, besides forming the solid basis of later Swedish law. How the laws could pass from one generation to another, without any codification, depends upon the fact that they were recited from memory by the justice (*lag-man* or *domare*), and that this dignity generally was inherited for centuries, being carried by the descendants of one and the same family. [a]

CHAPTER II
NORWAY IN THE NINETEENTH CENTURY

As early as 1790 negotiations took place between Count Armfeldt on behalf of Gustavus III of Sweden and various patriotic and influential Norwegians with a view to effecting a union between Norway and Sweden on equal terms, but the Norwegian negotiators expressed themselves unwilling to accept for Norway the government prevailing in Sweden. A minority of the patriots thought that the Danish yoke could only be broken by means of a union with Sweden, while a majority aimed at nothing less than absolute independence at any cost.

Such was the condition of Norway when by the treaty of Kiel (Jan. 14, 1814) the allies compelled the king of Denmark to cede Norway to Sweden and made Charles John Bernadotte crown prince of Sweden and Norway. The Norwegians denied the right of Denmark to Norway, refused to recognize the treaty of Kiel as having any binding force on them, as they were not parties to it, and invited Prince Christian Frederick of Denmark to accept the Norwegian throne from its people and to govern pursuant to a constitution adopted at Eidsvold, May 17, 1814. Among the provisions of this instrument are the following: That Norway should be a limited hereditary monarchy, independent and indivisible, whose ruler should be called a king; that all legislative power should reside in and be exercised by the people through their representatives; that all taxes should be levied by the legislative authority; that the legislative and judicial authority should be distinct departments; that the right of free press should be maintained; that no personal or hereditary distinction shall hereafter be granted to any one.

The election of a king and adoption of an independent constitution in disregard of the treaty of Kiel was tatamount to a declaration of war against Sweden, and as such it was taken. After the treaty of Paris and the abdication of Napoleon, the powers agreed to force Norway to accept the treaty of Kiel, and representatives of the allied powers came to Norway and demanded its compliance on penalty of war with the allies. The Norwegians remained obdurate. The Swedes, under Bernadotte, marched across the frontier and took the fortress Fredricksteen. Another division of the Swedish army was beaten by the Norwegians and driven back over the frontier. Several other engagements were fought, and it became evident that Norway could not be subdued without serious war. Sweden was exhausted by the wars of the allies against Napoleon and could ill endure more warfare. On Aug. 14, 1814, an armstice was declared, and it was provided that an extraordinary storthing should be called to settle the terms of permanent peace. By the terms finally agreed upon, Bernadotte was elected king of Norway under the title of Charles XIII, and he accepted the Norwegian constitution adopted at Eidsvold, May 17, 1814, and agreed to govern under and subject to its provisions. At the same time the Supreme Court of Norway was established in Christiania. The Bank of Norway was established at Thronedjem in 1816. At the death of Charles XIII, in 1818, Charles John ascended the throne of both countries as Charles XIV John.

On several occasions there was friction between the king and the Norwegian Storthing. At the treaty of Kiel the king had promised that Norway would assume a part of the Norwegian-Danish public debt; but as the Norwegians had never acknowledged this treaty, they held that it was not their duty to pay any part of the debt, and declared besides that Norway was not able to do so. But as the powers had agreed to help Denmark to enforce her claims, a compromise was effected in 1821, by which the Storthing agreed to pay three million dollars, the king relinquishing his civil list for a certain number of years. The same Storthing adopted the law abolishing the nobility in Norway. This step also was strongly opposed by Charles John, but as it had been adopted by three successive Storthings, the act under the constitution became a law in spite of any veto.

For a number of years there existed a want of confidence between the king and the Norwegian people. The king did not like the democratic spirit of the Norwegians, and the reactionary tendencies of his European allies had quite an influence upon his actions. In 1821 he proposed ten amendments to the constitution, looking to an increase of the royal power, among which was one giving the king an absolute instead of a suspensive veto; another giving him the right to appoint the presidents of the Storthing, and a third authorizing him to dissolve the Storthing at any time. But these amendments met the most ardent opposition in the Storthing, and were unanimously rejected.

When the Norwegians commenced to celebrate the anniversary of the adoption of the constitution (May 17), the king thought he saw in this a sign of a disloyal spirit, because they did not rather celebrate the day of their union with Sweden, and he forbade the public celebration of the day. The result of this was that "Independence Day" was celebrated with so much greater eagerness. The students at the university especially took an active part under the leadership of that champion of liberty, the poet Henrik

Wergeland, who died in 1845. The unwise prohibition was the cause of the "market-place battle" in Christiania, May 17, 1829, when the troops were called out, and General Wedel dispersed the crowds that had assembled in the market-place. There was also dissatisfaction in Norway because a Swedish viceroy (Statholder) was placed at the head of the government, and because their ships had to sail under the Swedish flag.

The French July Revolution of 1830, which started the liberal movement throughout Europe, also had its influence in Norway. Liberal newspapers were established at the capital, and the democratic character of the Storthing became more pronounced, especially after 1833, when the farmers commenced to take an active part in the elections. Prominent among them was Ole Gabriel Ueland. The king was so displeased with the majority in the Storthing of 1836 that he suddenly dissolved it; but the Storthing answered this action by impeaching the Minister of State, Lövenskiold, for not having dissuaded the king from taking such a step. Lövenskiold was sentenced to pay a fine; the king then yielded and reconvened the Storthing. He also took a step toward conciliating the Norwegians by appointing their countryman, Count Wedel-Jarlsberg, as viceroy. This action was much appreciated in Norway. During the last years of this reign there existed the best of understanding between the king and the people. Charles John's great benevolence tended to increase the affection of the people, and he was sincerely mourned at his death, March 8, 1844, at the age of eighty years.

Charles John was succeeded by his son, Oscar I, who very soon won the love of the Norwegians. One of his first acts was to give Norway her own commercial flag and other outward signs of her equality with Sweden. His father had always signed himself "King of Sweden and Norway"; but King Oscar adopted the rule to sign all documents pertaining to the government of Norway as "King of Norway and Sweden." During the war between Germany and Denmark, King Oscar gathered a Swedish-Norwegian army in Scania, and succeeded in arranging the armstice of Malmoe in 1848. The war broke out anew, however, the following year, and he then occupied northern Schleswig with Norwegian and Swedish troops, pending the negotiations for peace between Germany and Denmark. During the Crimean War, King Oscar made a treaty with England and France (1855), by which the latter powers promised to help Sweden and Norway in case of any attack from Russia. General contentment prevailed during the happy reign of King Oscar, and the prosperity, commerce, and population of the country increased steadily. These satisfactory conditions did not, however, result in weakening the national feeling, and the Storthing, in 1857, declined to promote a plan, prepared by a joint Swedish and Norwegian commission, looking to a strengthening of the union. After a sickness of two years, during which his son, Crown Prince Charles, had charge of the government as prince-regent, King Oscar I died in July, 1859, at the age of sixty years. He was married to Josephine of Leuchtenberg, daughter of Napoleon's stepson, Eugene Beauharnais.

Charles XV was thirty-three years old when he ascended the throne. The progress in the material welfare of the country continued during his reign, and, like his father, he was very popular with the Norwegians. Numerous roads and railroads were started, all parts of the country were connected by telegraph, and the merchant marine grew to be one of the largest in the world. In 1869 a law was passed providing for annual sessions of the Storthing instead of triennial as heretofore.

Charles XV died Sept. 18, 1872, and, having no sons, was succeeded by his younger brother, Oscar II, the late ruler of Sweden. The Storthing appropriated the necessary funds for the expense of the coronation at Throndhjem (July 18, 1873), while the king sanctioned the bill abolishing the office of Statholder. But soon differences between the Storthing and the ministry brought on sharp conflicts. Long before Norway deposed King Oscar II (June 7, 1905), disruptions and war would doubtless have occurred had it not been for the wisdom and tact of the king. The last straw that broke the camel's back in this instance was the refusal of separate consular representation for Norway. The basis of this last demand was not mainly the commercial value to Norway of having its distinct consuls, though this was an element, but the right of Norway as a nation entirely independent of Sweden to be represented as such in its commercial relations with foreign nations. Sweden and Norway are now not only two distinct nations, but are competitors in trade and commerce. Norway's shipping and carrying trade far exceeds that of Sweden. The Norwegians have always been a seafaring people, and Norwegian sailors and marines are found in large numbers in the commercial marine and navies of all Europe and America. From the standpoint of Norway, common justice demanded that Norwegian merchants and sailors should, like every other nation, have their own consuls to represent and protect them in foreign countries.

Not being able to secure the approval of the king for separate consular representation, the Storthing, on June 7, 1905, passed resolutions declaring the dissolution of the union between Norway and Sweden, and that King Oscar had ceased to be the ruler of Norway. In the place of the king, the Storthing appointed the members of the Norway Council of State to act as a temporary government for the nation. The Storthing further declared that Norway had no ill feeling against King Oscar or his dynasty of Sweden, and asked the king to cooperate in selecting one of his own house to be king of Norway.

The Riksdag of Sweden met in extraordinary session, June 21, 1905, at the call of King Oscar, to consider the action of the Norwegian Storthing in declaring the dissolution of the union between the two countries. The opening of the session was marked by the usual ceremonial pomp, but also by a gravity and solemnity befitting the unusual occasion. The emotional feeling was intense and repressed with difficulty by both speakers and audience. The king, in his address to the Riksdag, maintained with dignity that he had acted within his constitutional rights and that Norway had not the power to dissolve the union which legally could be effected only by mutual consent. Nevertheless, it was with great sadness that he now urged negotiations for the severance of the ties between the two nations, believing that "the union was not worth the sacrifice which acts of coercion would entail." The bill prepared by the government was immediately presented to the Riksdag. It was of the same tenor as the king's address, and asked for authorization to negotiate with the Norwegian Storthing for the establishment of a common basis for the settlement of the question involved in the separation of the two kingdoms. The bill encountered strong opposition, both in and out of the Riksdag. In the Senate it was referred to a committee of nine anti-government members, while in the lower house the composition of the corresponding committee was equally divided between the two opposing parties, with the addition of two independent members. The Riksdag authorized the government to negotiate a loan of $25,000,000 for works of defense, and declared the harbors of Stockholm, Karlskrona, Gothenburg, and Farosund to be war ports from which all foreign naval vessels were to be excluded. Norway's army was also mobilized and brought near the Swedish boundary.

Notwithstanding these warlike aspects, a peaceful dissolution of the union between Sweden and Norway was finally effected. The conference at Karlstad between the representatives of the two nations, on Sept. 23, 1905, drew up a protocol which became a treaty when subsequently ratified by the Riksdag and the Storthing, on the ninth of the following October. Thereupon Sweden canceled the charter of 1815 which governed the union of the two countries, and King Oscar declared Norway to be again separate and independent. Thus were severed the political relations between two countries, which, during a period of ninety years, had led to ever-increasing discord.

King Oscar II of Sweden steadfastly refused, however, to allow any prince of his house to be chosen as the new king of Norway, and the choice finally fell upon Prince Charles of Denmark, who was elected by an overwhelming majority at the plebiscite held throughout Norway on Nov.

12, 1905. He accepted the throne offered him and was crowned June 22, 1906.

The idea is prevalent that there is ill will between the Norwegian and Swedish peoples. This is a popular misconception. The Norwegian and Swedish peoples are racially very similar in character and habits, and mutually respect each other. King Oscar was as beloved and honored in Norway as he was in Sweden, and deservedly so. The Norwegians felt proud of his character, life, and statesmanship. They appreciated his wisdom and moderation, and gave him full credit for his earnest conviction that he was right in his differences with the Norwegian government. And yet, the dissolution was a blessing to both countries concerned. So long as Norway and Sweden were united under one king, there would have been friction. In like manner the long union between Norway and Denmark was a continuous source of irritation, but after the dissolution they were the best of friends. It has been suggested that Russia has long had her eye on the ice-free harbors of the Norwegian coast and has coveted them; that she has built her railroads across Finland close up to the Norwegian frontier, and that there is trouble ahead for Norway, because she has isolated herself from Sweden, her natural protector. But we see in the division a Greater Scandinavia. There are now the three great Scandinavian nations, Norway, Sweden, Denmark, and it can be imagined that, so close of kin, any one of them would rush to arms in defense of the others. A united Norway and Sweden under one king brought constant bickerings; a separate Norway and Sweden can be of mutual help.[b]

CHAPTER III
SWEDEN IN THE NINETEENTH CENTURY

Leading up to the events of the nineteenth century in Sweden were centuries of splendid history, some points of which will be briefly touched upon to connect the present-day Sweden with the mediaeval state.

During the Folkung Dynasty, in the fourteenth century, the royal houses of Sweden and Norway became united through the marriage of Duke Eric, of Sweden, and Ingeborg, only child of King Haakon, of Norway; and Duke Valdemar to the king's niece of the same name. In May, 1319, King Haakon died, and Magnus Ericsson, the young son of Duke Eric and Princess Ingeborg, inherited the crown of Norway, and July 8 of the same year was elected King of Sweden, at Mora in Upland.

For the attainment of this end, Magnus' mother, Duchess Ingeborg, and seven Swedish councillors had worked with great activity. They had taken part in shaping the first Act of Union of the North in June, 1319, and from Oslo, in Norway, hastened to have Magnus elected at the Stone of Mora, where the Swedish kings since time immemorial were nominated. The Act of Union stipulated that the two kingdoms were to remain perfectly independent, the king to sojourn an equally long part of the year in each, with no official of either country to accompany him further than the frontier. In their foreign relations the countries were to be independent, but to support each other in case of war. The king was the only tie to bind them together.

There was another Magnus whose candidacy was spoiled by this union. He was the son of King Birger, already as a child chosen king of Sweden in succession to his father. Magnus Birgersson, a prisoner at Stockholm, was beheaded in 1320, to make safe the reign of his more fortunate cousin. King Magnus was only three years old, and Drotsete Mattias Kettilmundsson presided over the government during his minority, the nobles of the state council having great power and influence. Both in Sweden and Norway the nobility had by this time attained a supremacy which was oppressive both to the king and the people, not so much through their privileges as through the liberties they took. Their continual feuds between themselves disturbed the peace of the country.

In 1332, King Magnus took charge of the government. He was a ruler of benign and good disposition toward the common people, whose interests he always furthered. But he lacked strength of character, and was not able to control the obnoxious nobles. The provinces of Scania and Bleking suffered greatly under Danish rule, which was changed into German oppression when handed over to the counts of Holstein as security for a loan. The people of Scania rose in revolt and asked for protection from King Magnus. At a meeting in Kalmar, in 1832, both provinces were united to Sweden. But the king had to pay heavy amounts in settlement, which were increased when Halland was procured in a similar way.

King Magnus was, at his zenith of power, one of the mightiest monarchs in Europe, having under his rule the entire Scandinavian peninsula and Finland, a realm stretching from the sound at Elsinore to the Polar Sea, from the river Neva to Iceland and Greenland. In 1335, King Magnus decreed that no Christian within his realm should remain a thrall, thus practically abolishing the remnants of slavery.

But financial difficulties arose, an unsuccessful crusade was attempted, the "Black Death" came from England to Norway in 1350 and spread with great rapidity, and several other things convened to fill the people with discontent, so that the union with Norway did not prove a happy one. A separation was brought about in 1844, when Haakon, the younger son of Magnus, was made king of Norway, Magnus remaining in power until Haakon came of age, and his older son, Eric, was chosen king or heir-apparent of Sweden. It seems that this division had been preconceived by King Magnus when he gave this older son the Swedish name of Eric and to the younger the Norwegian name of Haakon, both equally characteristic of the royal lines of the respective countries.

It was during the Folkung period that there flourished one of the most remarkable and renowned of Swedish women, St. Birgitta. At the Swedish court, she was the highest functionary of Queen Blanche, where she gathered deep and strong indignation against the mighty and powerful world. By some she is considered a reformer before Luther, because she insisted on direct communication between the communicant and God without the mediation of priests or saints. Yet there was a difference between Birgitta and Luther, because the latter sought to reform institutions, while the former would reform the upholders of the institutions.

After the reign of Magnus and his sons, there came for a brief season Albrecht of Germany, and after him Queen Margaret, who united for the first time in history the three Scandinavian countries and their dependencies. This period was denominated one of unionism against patriotism, and closed with the rebellion of Denmark and the ascending of the Swedish throne by Christian of Denmark, who claimed the right of his descent from St. Eric. Then followed the public execution under edict of King Christian, when eighty-two persons were beheaded, including many bishops and men of note in Sweden.

It is needless to say that this period was followed immediately by one of revolution and reformation, characterized by much heroism and patriotism, and bringing into prominence those splendid warriors, Gustavus Vasa, Gustavus Adolphus, Charles XII, and others, and the memorable battle of Pultowa and other lesser engagements.

After this came a period of political grandeur under various rulers, notably Queen Christine, followed by what has been called the period of Liberty, or the Aristocratic Republic, under Queen Ulrica Eleonore, when literature and the arts and sciences flourished, and Swedenborg, Linnaeus, Dahlin, Tegnér, and many others came into prominence.

One of the most loved rulers of this period was Gustavus III. By his influence a revolution similar to that in France was put down, for which, at a mask ball in the Royal Opera, he was assassinated by conspiritors. It is true, historians tell us, that he was superficial, that he violated the law, had no regard for a constitutional government, and led the people into adventurous and expensive wars. Yet his noble patriotism, frank heroism, brilliant genius, and great generosity compelled the love of his countrymen. In this mixture of patriotism and universal cosmopolitanism, true genius and superficiality, earnestness and recklessness in the character of Gustavus III, the Swedes recognized peculiarities of their own national temperament, for which they love him dearly, and Tegnér has voiced this love in a few lines of his eulogy:

> There rests o'er Gustav's days a golden shimmer,
> Fantastic, foreign, frivolous, if you please;
> But why complain when sunshine caused the glamour?
> Where stood we now if it were not for these?
> All culture on an unfree ground is builded,
> And barbarous once the base of patriotism true;
> But wit was planted, iron-hard language welded,
> The song was raised, life more enjoyed and shielded,
> And what Gustavian was, is, therefore, Swedish too.

On his death-bed, Gustavus III appointed his brother Charles and Charles Gustavus Armfelt members of the government during the minority of his son. Gustavus IV Adolphus was declared of age and took charge of the government when eighteen (in 1796). His guardians retired, and the new monarch ruled alone, without favorites or influential advisers. This proved most unfortunate for Sweden, for he was entirely without the gifts of a regent. He was a lover of order, economy, justice, and pure morals, but through lack of mental and physical strength his good qualities were misdirected. His father's tragic fate had a sinister effect upon his mind, the equilibrium of which was also shaken by the outrages of the revolutionists in France. Of a morbid sensibility, and without inclination to confide in any one, his religious mysticism led him into a state close to insanity. He imagined himself to be the reincarnation of Charles XII, while in Napoleon he recognized the monster of the Apocalypse, which he himself was sent to fight and conquer.

He refused any alliance with Russia and Denmark, and stubbornly resisted the friendship France wished to bestow. By his imbecility he lost Finland to the kingdom, and was compelled to abdicate in 1808. This "lunatic monarch," as he was called, was escorted out of the country with his family, never to return, and died in St. Gallin, in 1837.

Under these conditions we find Sweden at the beginning of the nineteenth century, when Charles XIII was chosen to succeed his nephew, the abdicated Gustavus IV Adolphus. Charles XIII was one of the most unsympathetic of Swedish kings, but his reign marks a new period in Swedish history, commencing the era of constitutional government. The new constitution to which the king subscribed was not a radical document; it only reduced the power of the king. Hans Jaerta, one of the nobles who had renounced their privileges and been active in the conspiracy against Gustavus IV, was the leading spirit of the constitutional committee, and was appointed secretary of state in the new cabinet.

It was necessary to select an heir to the throne, as Charles XIII was childless, and Prince Christian August of Augustenborg was chosen, much in opposition to the nobles, who wanted the son of Gustavus IV.

The Prince of Augustenborg, who was Danish governor-general of Norway, accepted, and was adopted by the king, changing his name to Charles August. Beloved by the lower classes who had effected his selection, he was treated coldly by the Gustavian aristocrats, and reports of attempts to poison the heir-apparent were in circulation even before he arrived in Sweden. Prince Charles August himself said he had often been warned that he would die young of paralysis, but paid no attention to the warnings given him. During a parade of troops at Qvidinge, in Scania, he was suddenly seen to lose consciousness and dropped dead from his horse. A report that seemed to favor the supposition that death resulted from poison, threw the populace into a frenzy, and the stoning to death of Count

Fersen resulted. This occurred at the burial of the dead prince, when Count Fersen, as marshal of the realm, opened the procession. Approaching the church of Riddarholm, his carriage was pelted with stones, Fersen himself seeking shelter in various places, but being pursued by the mob and killed. Thus perished a man who, with Curt von Stedingk, had received the order of Cincinnatus from the hands of George Washington, and who once was so near saving Louis XVI and Marie Antoinette from their cruel fate. Fersen's brother was saved only by mere chance, and his sister by a flight in disguise.

Sweden was once more without an heir-apparent to the throne, and, though others had been proposed, King Charles sent two emissaries to Napoleon to notify him of the death of Charles August and the selection of his brother. Then one of the most original and daring schemes ever attempted on such a line was carried through by Count Otto Moerner, one of the emissaries. On his own responsibility, he inquired of Marshal Bernadotte, one of Napoleon's ablest generals, if he would consent to become heir-apparent to the Swedish throne. Bernadotte consented, and the consent of Napoleon was obtained through the Swedish ambassador in Paris. Upon his return, Moerner was ordered to leave the capital, by the minister of state, who blamed him for his unauthorized action. But, from Upsala, Moerner led an eager agitation, with the result that the Riksdag of Oerebro selected Bernadotte, who was represented by a secret emissary. Thus, the two generals who, at the abdication of Gustavus IV, were, one in Norway, the other in Denmark, with troops ready to attack Sweden, both within one year were chosen to succeed Charles XIII. And this is how the Bernadottes, the present reigning family of Sweden, came to the throne. Marshal Bernadotte took the name of Prince Charles Johann.

It was in 1818, four years after Norway had been joined to Sweden, that Charles XII died, at the age of seventy, and Charles XIV Johann, the first of the Bernadotte dynasty, succeeded him, at the age of fifty-four years. His reign was one of reconstruction—politically, financially, and socially,—and during the last years of his life he received strong and repeated evidence of the love of his people, especially upon the twenty-fifth anniversary as king of Sweden.

Oscar I, his son, was forty-five years of age at the death of his father. He did not possess his father's brilliant genius or power of personal influence, but was fondly devoted to the fine arts, himself a talented painter and composer. He was a hard worker, and also fond of the pleasures of life. His health was injured through illness, in 1857, and he never recovered. The premature death of his second son, Prince Gustavus, a talented composer and highly popular, had a disastrous effect on him, and he died July 8, 1859, after a long illness, beloved by the two nations who, during his reign, had enjoyed the happiest epoch of their history.

It was during the reign of the late king, Oscar II, that Sweden attained her greatest prosperity and made most progress. Oscar II, brother of his predecessor, ascended the throne at a moment when universal peace was restored after the great conflict between France and Germany, and when an age of commercial prosperity for Sweden seemed to have begun. King Oscar had received the same superior education as his older brothers, was as brilliantly gifted as they, and of a more scholarly mind. As a writer on scientific subjects, a poet, and an orator, Oscar II distinguished himself before his succession to the throne, and still he did not find it easy to gain the love and admiration of the Swedish people, of which he was so eminently worthy. He was the successor of one of the most popular rulers the country ever saw, and, though appreciation came slowly, he lived to see his own popularity almost outrival that of his predecessor. During the last years of his life he was considered the most learned and popular of the monarchs of Europe.

He showed great discernment in his arrangement of dynastic matters. Himself married to the fervently religious Princess Sophie of Nassau, the king brought about the marriage of his oldest son, Crown Prince Adolphus, the present king of Sweden, to Princess Victoria of Bade, a granddaughter of Emperor William of Germany, and a great-granddaughter of Gustavus IV of Sweden. His third son, Prince Charles, Duke of West Gothland, is married to Princess Ingeborg of Denmark, a granddaughter of Charles XV of Sweden. These unions are well calculated to accentuate the increasing political, commercial, and cultural intimacy with Germany, the Scandinavian policy of life predecessor, and the desire of King Oscar to see the descendants of the old royal line of Sweden as heirs to the crown. In giving his consent to the marriage of his second son, Prince Oscar, to Lady Ebba Munck, of the Swedish nobility, King Oscar gave evidence of the fact that he was not a matchmaker regardless of the feelings of the parties involved. Prince Oscar, formerly Duke of Gothland, upon renouncing his share of inheritance to the throne of Sweden, also the throne of Norway, for the two kingdoms were then united, was allowed to marry the choice of his heart. King Oscar also tried to heal the wounds of the past by opening the vaults of the church of Riddarholm to the sarcophagi of Gustavus IV, the exiled king, and his son, and by giving Queen Carola of Saxony, the only living granddaughter of Gustavus, repeated proofs of esteem and considerate distinction.

King Oscar with his two crowns received as an inheritance two important problems to be solved—the reorganization of the Swedish army and the settlement of the difficulties between Norway and Sweden. How he handled the latter has been told about in the preceding chapter. The reorganization of the Swedish army was not effected until after twenty years of parliamentary struggle, but is now, thanks to the energies and perseverance of King Oscar, on a solid basis.

During the nearly one hundred years of peace which Sweden has enjoyed under the rule of the Bernadotte dynasty, she has developed her constitutional liberty and her material prosperity in a high degree. The dreams of glory by conquest belonged to the days gone by, but in the fields of peaceable industries she has attained a greatness which the world begins to realize. At the expositions of Paris in 1867, 1878, and 1889, of Vienna in 1873, of Philadelphia in 1876, and of Chicago in 1893, Swedish industry and art have taken part with honor in the international competition. The railways of Sweden have incessantly spun a more and more extended network of steel over the country, opening connections for enterprises in new districts, and furthering commerce and industrial art in a wide measure.

In all this advancement, King Oscar took a lively initiative, and that his policy will be continued by his successor, who has been so short a time on the throne, is not to be doubted, since the reins of government were in his hands practically long before the death of his father, who for several years suffered ill health. To say the least, Sweden, in the nineteenth century, played an important part in the strengthening of the great Scandinavian amalgamation, Norway, Sweden, and Denmark, which greets the twentieth century,[c]

CHAPTER IV
THE RELIGION OF THE NORTHMEN

The religion of the ancient Norwegians was of the same origin as that of all other Germanic nations, and, as it is the basis of their national life, a brief outline of it will be necessary in these pages.

In the beginning of time there were two worlds: in the South was Muspelheim, luminous and flaming, with Surt as a ruler; in the North was Niflheim, cold and dark, with the spring Hvergelmer, where the dragon Nidhugger dwells. Between these worlds was the yawning abyss Ginungagap. From the spring Hvergelmer ran icy streams into the Ginungagap. The hoarfrost from these streams was met by sparks from Muspelheim, and by the power of the heat the vapors were given life in the form of the Yotun or giant Ymer and the cow Audhumbla, on whose milk he lives. From Ymer descends the evil race of Yotuns or frost-giants. As the cow licked the briny hoarfrost, the large, handsome and powerful Bure came into being. His son was Bur, who married a daughter of a Yotun and became the father of Odin, Vile, and Ve. Odin became the father of the kind and fair Aesir, the gods who rule heaven and earth.

Bur's sons killed Ymer, and in his blood the whole race of Yotuns drowned except one couple, from whom new races of Yotuns or giants descended. Bur's sons dragged the body of Ymer into the middle of Ginungagap. Out of the trunk of the body they made the earth, and of his blood the sea. His bones became mountains, and of his hair they made trees. From the skull they made the heavens, which they elevated high above the earth and decorated with sparks from Muspelheim. But his brain was scattered in the air and became clouds. Around the earth they let the deep waters flow, and on the distant shores the escaped Yotuns took up their abode in Yotunheim and in Utgard. For protection against them the kind gods made from Ymer's eyebrows the fortification Midgard as a defense for the inner earth. But from heaven to earth they suspended the quivering bridge called Bifrost, or the rainbow.

The Yotun woman Night, black and dark as her race, met Delling (the Dawn) of the Aesir race, and with him became the mother of Day, who was bright and fair as his father. Odin placed mother and son in the heavens, and bade them each in turn ride over the earth. Night rides ahead with her horse Hrimfaxe, from whose foaming bit the earth is every morning covered with dew. Day follows with his horse Skinfaxe, whose radiant mane spreads light and air over the earth.

A great number of maggots were bred in Ymer's body, and they became gnomes or dwarfs, little beings whom the gods gave human sense and appearance. They lived within the mountains, and were skilful metal-workers, but they could not endure the light of day. Four dwarfs, the East, West, North, and South, were placed by the gods to carry the arch of heaven.

As yet there were no human beings on earth. Then, one day, the three gods, Odin, Keener and Lodur, were walking on the shore of the sea, where they found two trees, and from them they made the first man and the first woman, Ask and Embla (ash and elm). Odin gave them life, Hoener reason, Lodur blood and fair complexion. The gods gave them Midgard for a home, and from them the whole human race is descended.

The evergreen ash tree Ygdrasil is the finest of all trees. It shoots up from three roots. One of them is in the well Hvergelmer in Niflheim, and on this the dragon Nidhugger is gnawing. The other root is in Yotunheim, in the wise Yotun Mimer's fountain. One of Odin's eyes, which he pledged for a drink at this fountain, is kept here. Whoever drinks of this fountain becomes wise. The third root is in heaven, at the Urdar well, where the gods hold their Thing or court. To this place they ride daily over the bridge Bifrost. Here also the three Norns abide, the maidens Urd, Verdande, and Skuld (past, present, and future). They pour water from the well over the roots of the tree. The Norns distribute life and govern fate, and nothing can change their decision.

The dwelling in heaven of the Aesir or gods is called Asgard. In its middle was the field of Ida, the gathering-place of the gods, with Odin's throne, Lidskialv, from which he views the whole world. Odin is the highest and the oldest of the gods, and all the others honor him as their father. Odin's hall is Valhalla. The ceiling of this hall is made of spears, it is covered with shields, and its benches are ornamented with coats of mail. To this place Odin invites all who have fallen in battle, and he is therefore called Valfather, *i.e.*, the father of the fallen. The invited fallen heroes are called Einherier; their sport and pastime is to go out every day and fight and kill each other; but toward evening they awake to life again and ride home as friends to Valhalla, where they feast on pork of the barrow Saerimmer, and where Odin's maidens, the Valkyrias, fill their horns with mead. These Valkyrias were sent by Odin to all battles on earth, where they selected those who were to be slain and afterward become the honored guests at Valhalla. At Odin's side sit the two wolves, Gere and Freke, and on his shoulders the ravens, Hugin and Munin. These ravens fly forth every morning and return with tidings from all parts of the world. Odin's horse is the swift, gray, eight-footed Sleipner. When he rides to battle he wears a golden helmet, a beautiful coat of mail, and carries the spear Gungner, which never fails. Odin is also the god of wisdom and poesy; in the morning of time he deposited one of his eyes in pledge for a drink of Mimer's fountain of wisdom, and he drank Suttung's mead in order to gain the gift of poesy. He has also taught men the art of writing Runes and all secret arts.

Thor, the son of Odin, is the strongest of all the gods. His dwelling is called Thrudvang. He rides across the heavens in a cart drawn by two rams. He is always at war with the Yotuns or evil giants, and in battle with them he uses his great hammer, Mjolner, which he hurls at the heads of his enemies. The earth trembles under the wheels of his cart, and men call the noise thunder. Thor's wife is Sif, whose hair is of gold.

Balder is a son of Odin and Frigg. He is so fair that his countenance emits beams of brightness. He is wise and gentle, and is therefore loved by all. His dwelling is Breidablik, where nothing impure exists. Nanna is his wife.

Njord comes from the race of the wise Vanir. He rules the wind, can calm the seas and stop fire, and he distributes wealth among men. His aid is invoked for success in navigation and fishing. His wife is Skade, daughter of a Yotun, and his dwelling is Noatun by the sea.

Frey, the son of Njord, rules rain and sunshine and the productiveness of the soil, and his aid is needed to get good crops, peace and wealth. His dwelling is Alfheim. He sails in the magnificent ship Skibladner, which was built for him by the dwarfs. His wife is the Yotun daughter Gerd, but in order to get her he had to give away his good sword, so that he will be unarmed in the coming final battle of the gods.

Tyr, Odin's son, is the god of courage and victory, whom brave men call upon in battle. He has only one hand, for the Fenris-Wolf bit off his right hand.

Brage, the long-bearded, is the god of eloquence and poetry. His wife is Idun, who has in her keeping the apples of which the gods eat to preserve their eternal youth. Heimdal, the white god with teeth of gold, was in the beginning of time born by nine Yotun maidens, all sisters. He is the watchman of the gods. He is more wakeful than birds. He can see a hundred miles off, and he can hear the grass grow. His dwelling is Himinbjorg, which is situated where the Bifrost bridge reaches heaven. When he blows his

Gjallar-horn, it is heard throughout the world. Among the other gods were Haad, son of Odin, blind but strong; the silent and strong Vidar; Vale, the archer; Ull, the fast ski-runner, and Forsete, the son of Balder, who settles disputes between gods and men. Among the goddesses (or *asynier*), Frigg, Odin's wife, is the foremost. She knows the fate of everybody and shields many from danger. Her dwelling is Fensal. Next comes Freya, the goddess of love. She is the daughter of Njord and sister of Frey. She is also called Vanadis, or the goddess of the Vanir. She was married to Odd, and by him had a daughter Noss. But Odd left her, and Freya weeps in her longing for him, and her tears are red gold. When she travels, her wagon is drawn by two cats. The name of her dwelling is Folkvang. There were also a number of other goddesses, who were in the service of either Frigg or Freya.

Aeger, the ruler of the turbulent and stormy sea, is a Yotun, but he is a friend of the gods. When they visit him his hall is lighted with shining gold. His wife is Ran, and their daughters are the waves.

In the beginning there was peace among gods and men. But the arrival of the Yotun women in Asgard undermined the happiness of the gods, and in heaven and on earth a struggle commenced which must last until both are destroyed. The Yotuns continually attack the inhabitants of Asgard, and it is only the mighty Thor who can hold them at bay. It is the evil Loke, who is the worst enemy of gods and men. He belongs to the Yotun race, but was early adopted among the gods. He was fair in looks, but wily and evil in spirit. He had three evil children—the Fenris-Wolf, the Midgard-Serpent, and Hel. The gods knew that this offspring of Loke would cause trouble; therefore they tied the Fenris-Wolf, threw the serpent into the sea, and hurled Hel down into Niflheim, where she became the ruler of the dead. All who die from sickness or age are sent to her awful dwelling, Helheim. This is the origin of the saying, "Whom the gods love die young."

The greatest sorrow which Loke caused the whole world was that by deceit he caused the death of the lovely god, Balder. Then the gods took an awful revenge. They tied him to three stones, and over his head they fastened a venomous serpent, whose poison was always to drip upon his face. Loke's faithful wife, Sigyn, placed herself at his side and held a cup under the poisonous drip; but whenever the cup is full and she goes to empty it, the poison drips into Loke's face, and then he writhes in agony so that the whole world trembles. This is the cause of earthquakes.

There will come a time when these gods and the world shall perish in *Ragnarokk*, which means the perdition of the gods. They will have many warnings. Corruption and wickedness will be common in the world. For three years there will be winter without sun. The sun and the moon will be swallowed up by the wolves of the Yotuns, and the bright stars will disappear. The earth will tremble and the mountains will collapse, and all chains and ties are sundered. The Fenris-Wolf and Loke get loose, and the Midgard-Serpent leaves the ocean. The ship Naglfar carries the army of the Yotuns across the sea under the leadership of the Yotun *Rym*, and Loke advances at the head of the hosts from the abode of Hel. The heavens split, and the sons of Muspel come riding ahead, led by their chief Surt. As the hosts are rushing across the Bifrost, the bridge breaks with them. All are hastening to the great battlefield, the plains of *Vigrid*, which is a hundred miles wide. Now Heimdal arises and blows his Gjallar-horn, all the gods are assembled, the ash Ygdrasil trembles, and everything in heaven and on earth is filled with terror. Gods and Einherier (the fallen heroes) arm themselves for battle. In the front rides Odin with his golden helmet and beaming coat of mail and carrying his spear, Gungner. He meets the Fenris-Wolf, who swallows him, but Vidar avenges his father and kills the wolf. Thor crushes the head of the Midgard-Serpent, but is stifled to death by its venom. Frey is felled by Surt, and Loke and Heimdal kill each other. Finally Surt hurls his fire over the world, gods and men die, and the shriveling earth sinks into the abyss.

But the world shall rise again and the dead come to life. From above comes the all-powerful one, he who rules everything, and whose name no one dares utter. All those who were virtuous and pure of heart will gather in *Gimle* in everlasting happiness, while the evil ones will go to Naastrand at the well Hvergelmer to be tortured by Nidhugger. A new earth, green and beautiful, shall rise from the ocean. The gods awake to new life and join *Vidar* and *Vale*, and the sons of Thor, Mode and Magne, who have survived the great destruction and who have been given their father's hammer, because there is to be no more war. All the gods assemble on the field of Ida, where Asgard was located. And from *Liv* and *Livthraser*, who hid themselves in Ygdrasil during the burning of the world, a new human race shall descend. [d]

CHAPTER V
NORWEGIAN LITERATURE

The people who emigrated from Norway and settled in Iceland, after Harald the Fairhaired had subdued the many independent chiefs and established the monarchy (872), for the most part belonged to the flower of the nation, and Iceland naturally became the home of the old Norse literature. Among the oldest poetical works of this literature is the so-called "Elder Edda," also called "Saemund's Edda," because for a long time it was believed to be the work of the Icelander Saemund. "The Younger Edda," also called "Snorre's Edda," because it is supposed to have been written by Snorre Sturlason (born 1178, died 1241), contains a synopsis of the old Norse religion and a treatise on the art of poetry. Fully as important as the numerous poetical works of that period was the old Norse Saga-literature (the word saga means a historical tale). The most prominent work in this field is Snorre Sturlason's *Heimskringla*, which gives the sagas of the kings of Norway from the beginning down to 1777. A continuation of the *Heimskringla*, to which several authors have contributed, among them Snorre Sturlason's relative, Sturla Thordson, contains the history of the later kings down to Magnus Law-Mender.

The literary development above referred to ceased almost entirely toward the end of the fourteenth century, and later, during the union with Denmark, the Danish language gradually took the place of the old Norse as a book-language, and the literature became essentially Danish. Copenhagen, with its court and university, was the literary and educational center, where the young men of Norway went to study, and authors born in Norway became to all intents and purposes, Danish writers. But Norway furnished some valuable contributors to this common literature. One of the very first names on the records of the Danish literature, Peder Claussön (1545-1614), is that of a Norwegian, and the list further includes such illustrious names as Holberg, Tullin, Wessel, Steffens, etc.

One of the most original writers whom Norway produced and kept at home during the period of the union with Denmark was the preacher and poet, Peder Dass (1647-1708). The best known among his secular songs is

Nordlands Trompet, a beautiful and patriotic description of the northern part of Norway.

Ludvig Holberg was born in Bergen, Norway, Dec. 3, 1684. His father, Colonel Holberg, had risen from the ranks and distinguished himself, in 1660, at Halden. Shortly after his death the property of the family was destroyed by fire, and at the age of ten years Ludvig lost his mother. It was now decided to have him educated for the military service; but he showed a great dislike for military life, and, at his earnest request, he was sent to the Bergen Latin School. In 1702 he entered the University of Copenhagen. Being destitute of means, he took a position as private tutor. As soon as he had saved a small sum he went abroad. He was first in Holland, and afterward studied for a couple of years at Oxford, where he supported himself by giving instruction in languages and music. Upon his return to Copenhagen he again took a position as private tutor and had an opportunity to travel as teacher for a young nobleman. In 1714 he received a stipend from the king, which enabled him to go abroad for several years, which he spent principally in France and Italy. In 1718 he became regular professor at the Copenhagen University. Among Holberg's many works the following are the most prominent: *Peder Paars*, a great comical heroic poem, containing sharp attacks on many of the follies of his time; about thirty comedies in Moliere's style, and a large number of historical works. Holberg, who was ennobled in 1747, died in January, 1754, and was buried in Sorö Church. His influence on the literature and on the whole intellectual life of Denmark was very great. He is often called the creator of Danish literature.

Christian Baumann Tullin (1728-1765), a genuine poetical genius, who has been called the father of Danish lyrical verse, was born in Christiania, and his poetry, which was mainly written in his native city, breathes a national spirit. From his day, for about thirty years, Denmark obtained the majority of her poets from Norway. The manager of the Danish National Theater, in 1771, was a Norwegian, Niels Krog-Bredal (1733-1778), who was the first to write lyrical dramas in Danish. A Norwegian, Johan Nordal Brun (1745-1816), a gifted poet, wrote tragedy in the conventional French taste of the day. It was a Norwegian, Johan Herman Wessel (1742-1785), who by his great parody, *Kjaerlighed uden Strömper*, "Love without Stockings," laughed the French taste out of fashion. Among the writers of this period are also Claus Frimann (1746-1829), Peter Harboe Frimann (1752-1839), Claus Fasting (1746-1791), John Wibe (1748-1782), Edward Storm (1749-1794), C.H. Pram (1756-1821), Jonas Rein (1760-1821), and Jens Zetlitz (1761-1821), all of them Norwegians by birth. Two notable events led to the foundation of an independent Norwegian literature: the one was the establishment of a Norwegian university at Christiania, in 1811, and the other was the separation of Norway from Denmark, in 1814. At first the independent Norwegian literature appeared as immature as the conditions surrounding it. The majority of the writers had received their education in old Copenhagen, and were inclined to follow in the beaten track of the old literature, although trying to introduce a more national spirit. All were greatly influenced by the political feeling of the hour. There was a period when all poetry had for its subject the beauties and strength of Norway and its people, and *The Rocks of Norway, The Lion of Norway,* etc., sounded everywhere. Three poets called *Trefoil,* were the prominent writers of this period. Of these, Conrad Nicolai Schwach (1793-1860) was the least remarkable. Henrik A. Bjerregaard (1792-1842) was the author of *The Crowned National Song,* and of a lyric drama, *Fjeldeventyret,* "The Adventures in the Mountains." The third member of the *Trefoil,* Mauritz Christian Hansen (1794-1842), wrote a large number of novels and national stories, which were quite popular in their time. His poems were among the earliest publications of independent Norway.

The time about the year 1820 is reckoned as the beginning of the new Norwegian literature, and Henrik Wergeland is called its creator. Henrik Arnold Wergeland was born in 1808. His father, Nicolai Wergeland, a clergyman, was a member of the Constitutional Convention at Eidsvold. Henrik studied theology, but did not care to become a clergyman. In 1827, and the following years, he wrote a number of satirical farces under the signature *Siful Sifadda.* In 1830 appeared his lyric, dramatic poem, *Skabelsen, Mennesket og Messias,* (The Creation, Man and Messiah), a voluminous piece 'of work, in which he attempted to explain the historical life of the human race. As a political writer he was editorial assistant on the *Folkebladet* (1831-1833), and edited the opposition paper *Statsborgeren* (1835-1837). He worked with great zeal for the education of the laboring class, and from 1839 until his death edited a paper in the interest of the laborer. The prominent features of his earliest efforts in literature are an unbounded enthusiasm and a complete disregard of the laws of poetry. At an early age he had become a power in literature, and a political power as well. From 1831 to 1835 he was subjected to severe satirical attacks by the author Welhaven and others, and later his style became improved in every respect. His popularity, however, decreased as his poetry improved, and in 1840 he had become a great poet but had no political influence. Among his works may be named *Hasselnödder, Jöden,* "The Jew," *Jodinden,* "The Jewess," *Jan van Huysum's Blomsterstykke,* "Jan van Huysum's Flowerpiece," *Den Engleske Lods,* "The English Pilot," and a great number of lyric poems. The poems of his last five years are as popular to-day as ever. Wergeland died in 1845.

The enthusiastic nationalism of Henrik Wergeland and his young following brought conflict with the conservative element, which was not ready to accept everything as good simply because it was Norwegian. This conservative element maintained that art and culture must be developed on the basis of the old association with Denmark, which had connected Norway with the great movement of civilization throughout Europe. As the political leader of this "Intelligence" party, as it was called, appeared J.S. Welhaven.

John Sebastian Cammermeyer Welhaven was born in Bergen in 1807, entered the university in 1825, became a *Lector* in 1840, and afterward Professor of Philosophy. "His refined esthetic nature," says Fr. Winkel Horn, "had been early developed, and when the war once broke out between him and Wergeland, he had reached a high point of intellectual culture, and thus was in every way a match for his opponent." The fight was inaugurated by a preliminary literary skirmish, which was, at the outset, limited to the university students; but it gradually assumed an increasingly bitter character, both parties growing more and more exasperated. Welhaven published a pamphlet, *Om Henrik Wergelands Digtekunst og Poesie*, in which he mercilessly exposed the weak sides of his adversary's poetry. Thereby the minds became still more excited. The "Intelligence" party withdrew from the students' union, founded a paper of their own, and thus the movement began-to assume wider dimensions. In 1834, appeared Welhaven's celebrated poem, *Norges Daemring*, a series of sonnets, distinguished for their beauty of style. In them the poet scourges, without mercy, the one-sided, narrow-minded patriotism of his time, and exposes, in striking and unmistakable words, the hollowness and shortcomings of the Wergeland party. Welhaven points out, with emphasis, that he is not only going to espouse the cause of good taste, which his adversary has outraged, but that he is also about to discuss problems of general interest. He urges that a Norwegian culture and literature can not be created out of nothing and to promote their development it is absolutely necessary to continue the associations which have hitherto been common to both Norway and Denmark, and thus to keep in *rapport* with the general literature of Europe. When a solid foundation has in this manner been laid, the necessary materials for a literature would surely not be wanting, for they are found in abundance, both in the antiquities and in the popular life of Norway. Welhaven continued his effective work as a poet and critic. Through a series of romantic and lyrical poems, rich in contents and highly finished in style, he developed a poetical life, which had an important influence in the young Norwegian literary circles. He died in 1873.

Andreas Munch (1811-1884), an able and industrious poetical writer, took no part in the controversy between Wergeland and Welhaven, but followed his Danish models independently of either. His *Poems, Old and*

New, published in 1848, were quite popular. His best work is probably *Kongedatterens Brudefart*, "The Bridal Tour of the King's Daughter," 1861.

In the period of about a dozen years following the death of Wergeland, the life, manners, and characteristics of the Norwegian people were given the especial attention of literary writers. Prominent in this period was Peter Christian Ashbjornsen (1812-1885), who, partly alone and partly in conjunction with Bishop Jorgen Moe (1813-1882), published some valuable collections of Norwegian folk tales and fairy tales. Moe also published three little volumes of graceful and attractive poems. Among other writers of this period may be named Hans H. Schultz, N. Ostgaard, Harald Meltzer, M.B. Landstad, and the linguist Sophus Bugge.

The efforts to bring out the national life and characteristics of the people in literature also led to an attempt to nationalize the language in which the literature was written. The movement was the so-called *Maalstraev*, and had in view the introduction of a pure Norwegian book language, based upon the peasant dialects. The prominent supporter of this movement was Ivar Aasen (1813-1898), the author of an excellent dictionary of the Norwegian language. A prominent poetical representative of this school was Aasmund Olafson Vinje (1818-1870), while Kristofer Janson (born 1841) has also written a number of stories and poems in the *Landsmaal* (country tongue).

> A new and grand period in Norwegian literature
> commenced about 1857, and the two most conspicuous
> names in this period—and in the whole Norwegian
> literature—are those of Henrik Ibsen and Björnstjerne
> Björnson.

Henrik Ibsen was born in Skien, in 1828. He has written many beautiful poems; but his special field is in the drama, where he is a master. His first works were nearly all historical romantic dramas. His first work, *Catilina*, printed in 1850, was scarcely noticed until years afterward, when he had become famous. In 1856 appeared the romantic drama, *Gildet paa Solhaug*, "The Feast at Solhaug," followed by *Fru Inger til Oestraat*, 1857, and *Haermaedene paa Helgeland*, "The Warriors on Helgeland," 1858. In 1863, he wrote the historical tragedy *Kongsemnerne*, "The Pretenders," in which the author showed his great literary power. Before this play was published, he had been drawn into a new channel. In 1862, he began a series of satirical and philosophical dramas with *Kjaerlighedens Komedie*, "Love's Comedy," which was succeeded by two masterpieces of a similar kind, *Brand*, in 1866, and *Peer Gynt*, in 1867. These two works were written in verse; but in *De Unges Forbund*, "The Young Men's League," 1869, a political satire, he abandoned verse, and all his subsequent dramas have been written in prose.

In 1873 came *Keiser og Galilaeer*, "Emperor and Galilean." Since then he has published a number of social dramas which have attracted world-wide attention. Among them are: *Samfundets Stötter*, "The Pillars of Society," *Et Dukkehjem*, "A Doll's House," *Gengangere*, "Ghosts," *En Folkefiende*, "An Enemy of the People," *Rosmerholm, Fruenn fra Havet*, "The Lady from the Sea," *Little Eyolf, Bymester Solnes*, "Masterbuilder Solnes," *John Gabriel Borkman*, and the latest and most-talked-about, *Hedda Gabler*.

Björnstjerne Björnson (born in Osterdalen, in 1832) is the more popular of the two giants of Norwegian literature of to-day. His works are more national in tone. It has been said that to mention his name is to raise the Norwegian flag. His first successes were made in the field of the novel, and the first two, *Synnöve Solbakken*, 1857, and *Arne*, 1858, made his name famous. These, and his other peasant stories, will always retain their popularity. He soon, however, entered the dramatic field, and has since published a great number of dramas and novels.

In the field of belles-lettres there is at the present time a number of other talented authors. Jonas Lie (born 1833) has produced a number of excellent novels. Then there are Alexander Kielland (born 1849) Magdalene Thoresen (born 1819), Arne Garborg, Gunnar Heiberg, and a number of young authors.

In the field of science, also, modern Norway has a rich literature, with many prominent names, such as the historian Peter Andreas Munch (1810-1864), Johan Ernst Sars (born 1835), and O.A. Överland.[e]

CHAPTER VI
THE LITERATURE OF SWEDEN

Swedish literature is sublime and magnificent, like its history and its scenery; it is simple and glad, as well as sad, like the lives of its people. One of the great days in Sweden, or at least in Stockholm, is the celebration, on the 26th of July, of the anniversary of the birth, more than a century and a half ago, of the national poet Bellman.

His songs are as household words throughout the land. To the Stockholm born they speak of their daily life and surroundings, of the green isles and shady banks of the Malar, the flowery woods of Haga, the smiling park of Dijurgarden. Burlesque scenes of the life of the people, street tragedies, drinking bouts, and country junketings; broad humor and Nature's philosophy; lively fancies and exquisite landscape painting—such are the themes of his song, which from one generation to another has held the heart of the people spellbound. Every man, woman, and child knows his favorite ditties by heart, has sung or hummed them in moments of joy or sorrow. For his song is both joyful and sad. His joy is the joy of the simple hearted, his gladness a Dionysian gladness, the very enjoyment of existence; his sadness that of sympathy with suffering humanity, of anguish at the evanescence of life and happiness. His fancy oscillates between constant extremes and ever-recurring contrasts. It makes of his song, as Tegnér has so aptly defined it, "a sorrow decked in roses." Bright, gay, enraptured, full of sunshine and glamour, like the summer day around Stockholm, it is traversed by a strain of melancholy like a smile through tears, the laugh which conceals a sob. There is symbolism and there is parody in his rustic figures, but they are so living, so real, they appeal so strongly to the innermost feelings, that they seem the embodiment of one's thoughts. His pictures are like those of the Dutch painters: every trait in the rustic scene tells the life-story of some humble existence.

It is this characteristic which has made the poet appeal so powerfully to the minds of the people. He seems to see with their eyes and feel with their hearts, and to have experienced all the vicissitudes of their own life. And yet he eminently reflects his own time, the gay, the light-hearted Gustavian era, with its classical fancies and rococo tastes. Venus and Bacchus, the

Nymphs and the Dryads, Hebe and Amor are mixed up incongruously with the homely scenes of Scandinavian life. His Dutch pictures assume then a Watteau-like coloring of extraordinary effect, as fancy and contrast enhance the sharp outlines of his figures and give their vitality still greater relief. They are so lifelike and so various that the whole of the every-day life of Sweden, and more especially of Stockholm, of the eighteenth century, is unrolled before our eyes. It is said that if every other book descriptive of the period were to fail, his verses would suffice to inform us how the middle classes then lived, thought, and felt. Around the poet's monument—his bust in bronze on a white marble column—there gather, on the anniversary of his birth, the crowds who love him and love his song. Every heart beats high as the Bellman choirs burst forth in turn into the well-known melodies, composed or adapted by the poet himself to his words, and sung by him to the accompaniment of his lute. And song alternates with enthusiastic orations, addressed to the crowd by improvised orators, teeming with quotations of well-known lines. It is an orgy of Bellman's verse, such as the Stockholmer specially delights in. Bellman's songs generally form a sequence, a continuous chain of lyrical romance. His *Fredman's Epistles* are a sort of epic cycle of lyrics. This is a form often adopted by Swedish poets. We find it in Tegnér's *Frithiof's Saga*, in Runeberg's *Sayings of Sergeant Stal*, and in the works of other poets. It is a question, however, whether even by these Master Singers, in their more elaborate conceptions and genial flights of poetry, Bellman has ever been surpassed. In lyric power and vivid realism, his popular ditties are unrivaled.

The next to incarnate the genius of the Scandinavian race was Tegnér. His love of brave deeds and reckless adventure and his exaltation of the man of action above the man of thought are typical. His heroes, fair-haired and blue-eyed, stalwart and vigorous, relying on strength and longing for adventure, tender-hearted and contemplative when not aroused to violent action and bent on deeds of valor, personify the national ideal. His whole vision of life is Scandinavian, bright and vivid, with a tinge of melancholy. Tegnér was, with Geijer and Ling, the first to adopt national subjects, to use the Scandinavian myths and folk-lore in their poetry, in opposition to the classical themes and the Hellenic mythology, until then exclusively in vogue in the poetical field.

Geijer was a romantic by nature, in politics as well as in literature, but he was above all an ardent Scandinavian, opposed to exotics, and passionately devoted to the great traditions of the past, a hero-worshiper, an enthusiast, and a *Goth*. The Goths were members of a society formed to revive the old national manners and customs, the freedom of the age of the Vikings, and the ardor of the heroes of Walhalla. Their organ was the

Idun, an exclusively literary publication. In a letter written by Geijer from Stockholm to his *fiancee*, then living in the country, dated March 7, 1811, he says: "We have formed a society which meets nearly daily. We talk, smoke, and read together about Gothic Viking deeds. We call each other by Gothic names, and live in the past." And Anna-Lisa, his future wife, writing to a friend, says: "My *fiancee* has become a Goth; instead of loving me, he is in love with Valkyries and shield-bearing maidens, drinks out of Viking horns, and carries out Viking expeditions—to the nearest tavern. He writes poems which must not be read in the dark, they are so full of murders and deeds of slaughter." Ling, who also belonged to this society, was a fervent admirer of the Eddas and Sagas, of the Scandinavian myths and folk-lore. Tegnér, despite his classical education and Hellenic turn of mind, was an ardent Norseman in feeling and instinct. "Go to Greece for beauty of form," he would say, "but to the North for depth of feeling and thought." He scorned alike the metaphysical subtleties of French philosophy and the moonshine heroics of German romanticism. But he was at one with Geijer and Ling in the desire to make Scandinavian heroes and myths the subjects of poetry.

The result of the movement was *Frithiof's Saga*, by Tegnér, Geiger's *Viking*, and Ling's heavy epics of Walhalla warriors. But Geijer and Ling alone had followed out the theory in all its consequences. Their heroes were simply *Eddic*, of their time, in spirit and in thought. Ling's realism went so far that his Northern gods and warriors, "everlastingly killed but to revive again," were deemed "pork-eating and mead-drinking yokels." They were soon forgotten, and Ling himself is best known as the inventor of gymnastic exercises on scientific principles, an art now practiced all the world over as "Swedish gymnastics." Geijer, whose *Viking* gave a pure and true picture of Viking life seen in its own light, was himself disappointed. He abandoned poetry and took to history, though Tegnér says of him that if he had devoted himself to poetry, he would have surpassed all his contemporaries. As historian he rose to the highest rank; and he is perhaps the greatest historian Sweden has ever produced.

Tegnér had modernized his hero and heroine in *Frithiof's Saga*. He gave them Viking garbs and surroundings, but modern thoughts and sentiments. By the more copious development of the inner life, and by placing woman on an equality with man, love had received a higher meaning, and his poetry unfolded inspirations unknown to the ancient world, such as melancholy and the love of nature. He did no more than Tennyson did later in making of King Arthur the type of an English gentleman. Frithiof and Ingeborg were representatives of the national ideal. The success of his poem was immense. It had a lyrical intensity which set the Scandinavian mind vibrating. Unmindful of the anachronism, youth gloried in the noble disinterestedness of Frithiof, in his generosity to his rival, his melancholy philosophising and his high-minded love, as well as in his daring and his love of adventure. Manly breasts heaved in sympathy with him, and women's tears flowed at the story of Ingeborg's love. As the poet Snolisky has said —

> From the highest to the lowest throughout the land
> The poet had created a bond of union.
> In every home, within every school door,
> His verses were read and conned and loved,
> And Sweden's youth felt its cheek glow
> At Frithiof's courage and manly mood.
> While Ingeborg's love to the maiden's dream
> Gave life and thoughts to her weaving and sewing.

In his *Children of the Lord's Supper*, so beautifully translated for us by Longfellow, Tegnér conveyed a true image of Sweden's religious life. The scene in the country church, decked out with flowers and evergreens for the solemn ceremony, the rustic boys and girls bowing and curtseying as they make their responses before the assembled congregation, and the attitude and words of the patriarchal pastor are all true to life. The somewhat declamatory tone of the oration is not less consistent with the character of the rural parson, the trend of Swedish religious thought, and the solemnity associated with these occasions.

It was in his patriotic war-songs, however, that Tegnér roused the greatest enthusiasm. His *Svea*, his dithryambic declamation *King Charles*, and his *Scanean Reserves*, sent a thrill through young and old. When *Svea* was read at the Swedish Academy, which awarded the poem its gold medal, the friends and opponents of Tegnér alike were moved to undisguised admiration. In breadth and intrinsic power, and in the beauty of its rythm, which seems to echo the clash of arms and the marching of masses, this poem is unequalled in Swedish literature. Tegnér's name soon became known far beyond the limits of the lands where his language is understood. His works were translated into almost all modern tongues, so that some fifty different translations of the whole or parts of his poems now exist in eleven European languages.

A new feature was introduced into Swedish poetry by Runeberg. Although born of Swedish parents, he was brought up in Finland, his mind being nurtured in the traditions and the mixed racial influences of his new fatherland. Thus he breathed a new spirit, and a new inspiration, drawn from the realities of life, into poetical fiction. He was a realist in the best sense of that much-misused word. He sought his ideals *in* life, instead of outside of it and above it in imaginary creations. He saw nature such as it is, with all its faults and sublimities, and, loving it with a true poet's devotion, he painted it simply and faithfully, without aiming at ennobling it, but seeking and finding what there is of native dignity in its humblest expressions. In his lyrical poem, *The Sayings of Sergeant Stal*, he portrayed incidents of the wars of Finland fighting by the side of Sweden in 1809, when the country was conquered by Russia. It was a series of war pictures, a collection of hero types, painted in living colors, and breathing the most ardent patriotism.—Simple tales told by a sergeant of his recollections of the war, they deal with real personages, most of them drawn from the humblest stations in life, described just as they really lived and spoke and acted. Yet throughout the story of their simple acts and thoughts there swept a breeze which kindled the blood, roused the emotions; and fired the patriotic feeling of Runeberg's contemporaries. In poetic depth and beauty of language, as in style and conception, and in their departure from all the prevailing ideas and methods of romanticism, these lyric tales were a revelation. They classed their author at once as in the line of true-born poets. The works of Runeberg, although properly belonging to the literature of a country politically no longer one with Sweden, have from the nature of their subjects and the identity of languages, always been looked upon in Sweden as common property, and they have certainly exercised a powerful influence on Swedish thought and letters. Some of his songs, set to music, are to this day sung as national anthems.

The last champion of dying romanticism was a sort of universal genius, eccentric, *bizarre*, unequal, a spirit out of harmony with itself, but gifted with the most wonderful imagination and power, K.J.L. Almquist. His life was as checquered as his writings were various. In turn a clergyman, a schoolmaster, a journalist, and an exile, he has written volumes on almost every conceivable subject, from fiction, poetry, and history, to lexicography, pedagogy, and mathematics. His stories, published in two series, under the common title of *The Book of the Hedgerose*, show powers of conception, imagination, and description such as are only to be found in Edgar Allen Poe. His was an essentially revolutionary temperament. He disdained all authority, and cavilled at all moral restraints. He was in constant rebellion against society, its accepted laws and precepts, and vented his moral skepticism in bitter sarcasm and cutting paradoxes. "But two things are white in this world," he would say, "innocence and arsenic." The coupling of the two, however, nearly proved fatal to him. He was involved in a mysterious affair of poisoning, in which the victim was a dunning creditor. He was suspected of having given him arsenic by way of ridding himself of the debt which he could not pay. No proof of the fact could be adduced, and the crime was never brought home to him; but public opinion was against him, and fearing or distrusting the justice of his country, he fled from it ere the case was tried. He wandered over Europe and America, trying his hand at everything, and died, a literary wreck, in Germany, longing, and yet not daring, to return to his country. Lately, the Society of Authors in Stockholm, judging that his crime was "not proven," while his literary merits were great beyond all doubt, undertook the rehabilitation of his memory. His remains were brought back from Lubeck, and buried in Stockholm with "literary" honors, among others a remarkable oration delivered at his grave by Verner von Heidenstam, in which he was styled a martyr in the great cause of the emancipation of thought. Whatever may be thought of his moral character, Almquist was a great thinker and a wonderfully versatile writer. The last of the romantics, he has been called a realist, a psychologist, and a symbolist, and he was certainly something of all these, half a century before the terms became battle-cries in literature, and came to designate literary schools. One critic has made him out to have been a sort of forerunner of Ibsen, while another calls him the most modern of classics. His genius placed him in advance of his age in most things. He was the first in the list of those Scandinavian revolutionists who have laid out new landmarks in the field of thought, and introduced new methods in fiction and the drama.

Liberalism, which spread like wildfire over Europe after its outbreak in the July Revolution in France, reached Sweden soon after. It was represented in literature by such men as Sturzen-Becker, Wetterbergh, and Strandberg, writing under the names of Orvar Odd, Uncle Adam, and Talis-Qualis; Blanche, who wrote stirring novels in the style of Eugene Sue; Hjerta, and the staff of the then newly founded *Aftonbladet*, who were revolutionizing the press. The press was beginning to enlist the highest literary capacities of the country, gradually becoming what it now is, a purveyor not only of news but of thought, and a leader of opinion in literature and art, in science and philosophy. In poetry, liberalism found its echo in the verses of Malmström, Nybom, Schlstedt. In fiction its banner was carried by three women, two of whom—well known in England and America—Frederica Bremer, whose novels portrayed the home life of the middle class, Emelie Carlen, who idealized the fishermen and sea-faring folk of the West Coast, and Sophie von Knorring, who gave rather stilted descriptions of life in aristocratic circles. All three were very productive, and their novels count by dozens. Yet they failed to sustain the reputations their first works had won for them.

Verner von Heidenstam is now foremost among the writers of his country. His early works, *Endymion, Hans Alienus,* and others, raised him to this rank, and his last two productions, *The Carolines* (the companions of Charles XII) and *Saint Brigitt,* have more than confirmed it. *Hans Alienus* was, like Goethe's *Faust*, a work of deep philosophical research into the problems of existence, the purpose and significance of life, set forth in symbolical images and explained by allegory. In the *Carolines*, a series of short stories connected by the red thread of history which runs through them, he gives a new conception, but a wonderfully graphic and striking one, of Charles XII and his times. It is an epic, and yet so living and so human a picture of the wild, iron-souled, quick-tempered hero, whose "eyes flew around like two searching bees," and whose will was like the steel of his sword; who had the heart of a lion and a "woman's hatred for women," but for whom men shed their blood freely; who "never grieved over a misfortune longer than the darkness lasted," and was "best loved by those who tried to hate him." His pictures are drawn by a master hand, and with the intuitive coloring of genius. *Saint Brigitt* carries us back to medieval Sweden. Here, too, the picture is lifelike, centered round the struggle of a high-minded woman, who makes everything bend to her stern rule of holiness, her thirst for sanctity, as Charles XII did to his inexorable policy and thirst for dominion.

The psychological and the historical novel, the latter, in its modern conception, akin to the former, since it is a study of the psychology of historical characters and a historical epoch, is the form of fiction at present most in vogue. It is in this form that such writers as Tor Hedberg, Per Hallström, and Axel Lundegard have made their reputations. Tor Hedberg's romances embody profound analysis of the inner workings of the soul, of the secret motives which, more or less consciously, determine a man's acts. In this line he ventures on the most difficult psychological problems. In his *Judas*, a scriptural romance from which he has drawn a drama, he attempts to solve the darkest psychological enigma that has puzzled humanity, viz., to analyze the motives which led Judas to betray his Master and become the typical traitor. The character he draws of him is original and striking, and departs entirely from the accepted tradition. But bold and subtle as the theory is, it is far from convincing. His Judas is a dark, brooding spirit, fierce and inharmonious, divided between extatic love and admiration of his Master and inward irresistible forces of hatred and revolt: a double nature, thirsting for freedom and love, yet predestined to evil, and led by fearful secret impulses to the accomplishment of his destiny and the fulfilment of his mission, necessary to the scheme of salvation. He rushes blindly to his fate while struggling in vain to escape it. But in the very act of betrayal, while obeying the command: "What thou doest, do quickly," his better nature triumphs for one instant and he falls on the neck of his Master and embraces Him. It is the Judas kiss which betrays his Lord. The last look of Jesus, however, showed him that he had been understood and forgiven. The detestation of humanity to the end of the world will be his expiation, but that look of Jesus has freed him.

Woman, represented by writers like Ellen Key, Selma Lagerlöf, Sophie Elkau, Alfhild Agress, Hilma Stanberg, and others, holds a high position in Swedish letters. Ellen Key is an essayist of virile power and argumentative breadth, of superior intellect and unfailing erudition. She is a fearless and unfailing champion of free thought, individualism, and woman's emancipation. As was said of Madame de Staël, her writings are "the most masculine productions of the faculties of woman." Selma Lagerlöf occupies as a novelist a position of her own. Her style and her manner in fiction are unique. Symbolism and allegory are blended in it with the most realistic pictures of everyday life. She thinks in parables, and describes realities, and the realities convey the moral teachings of parables. With something of the peculiar power of George Eliot in the delineation of character, she makes each humble life preach some great moral truth. Her latest book, *Jerusalem*, is one of extraordinary fascination, created quite a sensation in Sweden, and places Selma Lagerlöf quite among the foremost writers of the day.

It may in general be said of Swedish writers that they have a high idea of their calling. Few, if any, have accepted as their sole function the idealization of form. They hold mostly that the highest aim of art should be to teach and elevate, to destroy prejudice and conventionality, and indicate, in so far as it is possible, the solution of moral problems through the creative faculty of inspired productiveness. The wish to inculcate action, the energy that is born of enthusiasm, the chivalry that is inspired by high ideals and unselfish motives. Raised thus from the region of mere chronicles of human passions, of woman's frailty and man's baseness, and exercising themselves with the political, social, and religious problems of the day, these works of imagination have become, alongside the Press, a powerful factor in the development of modern thought.[f]

CHAPTER VII
GOVERNMENT AND POLITICS OF NORWAY AND SWEDEN

Only for the past three years has Norway had an independent political life, and so few changes in local government have so far been made under the new king that it will be profitable, in this chapter, to take up the government and political life as it existed under the united Constitutional Monarchy of Norway and Sweden. In fact, it is no different than at that time, except that each has its separate king. In internal rule, the two countries were always separate, except in matters that pertained to the common weal of both. Thus, the Swedish Minister of Foreign Affairs had charge of the United Kingdoms, and, as previously stated, this was the rock on which the Union finally split.

The constitution of Norway, like that of the United States, invests all power in the people, who are represented by their legislature and their judiciary, with the king as an executive to administer the laws passed by the one, and enforce the decrees of the other. When the two houses of Parliament disagree upon a measure, they sit in joint session, when it requires a vote of two-thirds to enact it, and the approval of the king is necessary. He is also required to promulgate all the acts of the legislature. Many Norwegian statesmen assert that the king has no veto power, but merely temporary authority to suspend a law pending the action of the people. If three successive parliaments, after three successive elections, pass a bill in exactly the same terms, it does not require the sanction of the king when it is passed the fourth time. Thus the people may exercise their sovereignty.

All edicts of the executive, all decisions of the court, and all resolutions of the legislature are proclaimed in the king's name, but the ministry is responsible to the legislature for the acts of the king, and if they are not approved, as in England, the ministry must resign and a new one be organized in sympathy with a majority of the parliament. The king may choose his own ministers, but they must represent the will of the people. They are called counsellors of state, are eight in number. Before the disunion, two of these eight counsellors were without portfolios, and resided alternately at Stockholm, while the other members presided over six executive departments in Christiania.

A record is kept of the meetings of the ministry by a permanent secretary, and the constitution requires that each minister shall express his opinion upon all questions brought up for consideration. He who remains silent is counted in the affirmative. No matter of business can be determined by the king without the advice of the ministry, unless an emergency demands a prompt decision, when he must take the responsibility of securing a ratification of his act. In the same manner the king may issue edicts of a provisional character in matters of commerce, finance, industrial activity, customs dues, police and military affairs during a recess of the parliament, subject to its approval within a limited time after reassembling.

The minister may act in the king's name in cases of emergency or during his absence from the country, subject to his approval. These conditions were adopted in earlier times, when the Norwegian legislature sat only once in three years and some such power was necessary, but now that there are annual and often semi-annual sessions, and they have a king of their own residing always in Norway, it is very seldom necessary for the executive power to exercise such responsibility.

The king appoints all the officials of the executive part of the government, all the officers of the army and navy, and all the clergymen in the established church, but exercises this power through his ministers. Dissenting congregations are not subject to government control, and may choose their own clergymen, although the latter are required to register an oath of allegiance and a pledge to obey the laws of the nation and fulfill their duties with fidelity and conscientiousness.

The king is the head of the established church, which is the Lutheran. He is also commander-in-chief of the army and navy, but can not increase or decrease the military establishment without the approval of the parliament. He has the right to declare war and conclude peace, but can not expend money for military purposes, not even for the national defense, without the consent of the legislature. The Norwegian constitution is silent concerning his authority to conclude treaties with foreign powers, and the question has never been raised. He conducts negotiations through his ministers and submits the result of their labors for the approval of parliament. He has the power to suspend the collection of customs duties temporarily until the parliament can meet to consider the matter, but it has very rarely been exercised.

The parliament is called the storthing, and is composed of one hundred and fourteen representatives, thirty-eight from the towns and seventy-six from the rural districts. It divides itself into two sections, known as the odelsthing and the lagthing. The members are elected for three years by an indirect and complicated system which is nearly the reverse of our own. The voters of each parish, which forms an election district, assemble at a given place and time and select delegates to a convention which chooses their representatives in the storthing, and, when the storthing meets, its one hundred and fourteen members select one-fourth of their own members, generally the most experienced and distinguished men, to constitute a senate, or upper chamber, called the lagthing, which exercises a sort of supervisory power over legislation.

The storthing sits for about six months every year. The members are paid $3 a day during the session and their traveling expenses. The presiding officer is chosen every four weeks, and can not succeed himself without an interval. The committees are appointed by a "selection committee" elected by ballot, and each committee chooses his own chairman. There is a rather novel rule requiring bills referred to committees to be assigned for consideration to the several members in rotation. Any member may introduce a bill modifying the constitution, but all other classes or measures must proceed from the government and the members of the lower house. Members of the upper house, or lagthing, are not permitted to propose ordinary legislation, on the theory that they should remain unprejudiced so as to exercise a judicial revision. Thus, bills must originate in the odelsthing, which, having passed them, sends them to the lagthing for its approval.

The financial officers of the government and the directors of the national bank are elected by the storthing, which appoints a committee every six months to revise and audit the accounts of officials who have to do with the disbursement or collection of money. When an irregularity or improper expenditure is discovered, the legislature is asked to decide whether the minister in charge of the department shall repay the sum from his own pocket and repair the damage that has been caused by one of his subordinates.

In the same manner the storthing regulates all loans, on the theory that the money belongs to the people. The members of the ministry may be impeached by the odelsthing for a violation of the constitution and tried before the lagthing and the supreme court.

The following eight executive departments are in charge of ministers:

1. For ecclesiastical matters and public instruction, which also has charge of charities, insurance companies, and matters relating to the relief of the people.

2. The department of justice.

3. The department of the interior, which has jurisdiction over everything that is not under the other departments.

4. The department of agriculture.

5. The department of public works.

6. The department of finances and customs.

7. The department of defense.

8. The revision of public accounts department.

For administrative purposes, Norway is divided into twenty districts, viz.: The cities of Christiania and Bergen and eighteen "Amts" or provinces, which coinside with the diocese of the church, and there is a very close relation between the ecclesiastical and the civil authorities. The chief magistrate in each of the counties, nominated by the king, is known as an "Amtmand." His duties are similar to those of the French prefects, although the theory of home-rule and self-government is carried into each county and each municipality and parish, where every magistrate is responsible to a council elected by the people from among their own number. They make the laws for the magistrate to administer. There are few countries in which the theory of self-government is carried to such an extent as in Norway. The sovereignty of the people is absolute and their rights are jealously guarded. Norway is divided into ecclesiastical parishes, which are the voting districts, as in England, and are governed in a similar way.

The Norwegian constitution of 1814, based upon the principle of popular self-government, declared these municipalities completely independent in the management of their own affairs, placing the administrative authority, with the power of taxation and the disbursement of revenues in the hands of the taxpayers and householders, so that they could not be coerced by the national government, if there ever was any disposition in that direction.

This authority is exercised through a council called a "bystyre," composed of from twelve to forty-eight members, according to the population of the parish, who are elected for terms of three years, and serve gratuitously. The council elects from its own number a chairman who is the head of the whole municipal organization, and is known as an *ordförer*. He corresponds to the German burgomaster and the mayor of the American city.

In addition to the popular council there is a magistrate representing the royal government, who, with the consent of the council, may be admitted to their deliberations, but is not allowed to vote. He is also ex-officio a member and often chairman of the municipal departments or commissions, such as the board of public works, the school board, the harbor commission. In this way he becomes a connecting link between the national authority at Christiania and the municipal councils throughout the kingdom, because certain measures of local interest are subject to restrictions by the national parliament, particularly those involving finances.

Under the direction of the council are permanent executive departments similar to those found in the United States, pertaining to public highways, the public buildings, the public health, the relief of the poor, the fire department, police department, etc. These in every case are managed by permanent officials under the supervision of committees of the council. Every year a budget is made up of the income and expenditures expected; each department being permitted to submit its own estimates, which are approved or amended by the council, and the amount is raised by taxation of houses, lands, personal property, and incomes, with fees for licenses to transact business. The entire system of local taxation is similar to our own, and the methods of assessment are the same. In order to meet the expense of unusual undertakings for the benefit of the municipality, such as waterworks, tramways, docks, etc., funds are raised in the usual manner by the issue of interest bearing bonds, which are usually in small denominations in order to permit people of limited means to invest in them. They are redeemed, as a rule, in forty annual instalments, the bonds to be canceled being selected by lot. In this system of local government women now participate upon an equal basis with men.

With the exception of the British parliament, the Swedish riksdag is the oldest legislative body in the world. The kingdom of Sweden has maintained its integrity for not less than four thousand years. So far back as the anthropologists can trace the history of Swedish people, the boundaries of their land have remained the same. The Duchy of Finland was subject to Swedish sovereignty at one time, and at different times Sweden has been united with Norway and Denmark under the same ruler, but Sweden has been Sweden ever since human beings inhabited its territory, and it is the only nation in Europe that has never been conquered or had its boundaries changed by foreign powers. Since the beginning of history, home rule has prevailed among the people and has been defended and recognized as their right. The parishes have always controlled their own affairs, and since the Reformation their government has been in the hands of a board or council elected by the people, of which the pastor of the church is chairman. Everybody who pays taxes, men and women alike, may vote at the election of the council. The burgomaster serves for life, and is usually required to abstain from all other business except that which pertains to the public weal. The parishes are consolidated into twenty-four provinces, similar to our states, each having a certain independence and government of its own, although the governor-general, who also serves for life on good behavior, is appointed by the king. The city of Stockholm is an independent jurisdiction like the District of Columbia, with a governor appointed by the king. The riksdag was formerly composed of four distinct bodies,—nobles, clergymen, burghers, peasants,—representing the different classes of the community, and all laws required their approval. In 1866, however, this clumsy arrangement was abolished and the national legislature was consolidated into two bodies known as the first and second chamber, similar to our Senate and House of Representatives. The two chambers are equal in every respect, except that the second chamber, or lower house, has the advantage of numbers when a deadlock arises and the question in dispute is decided by a joint ballot. Then, unless there should be an overwhelming difference of opinion, the second chamber usually has its will, which is perfectly right, because it represents the people. The king must approve all legislation to make it effective, and his veto is final, except in matters concerning taxation and the expenditure of public money. The diet has the sole power to levy taxes and make appropriations with or without his consent.

The first chamber, which corresponds to our Senate, is composed of one hundred and fifty members, elected for terms of nine years by the provincial councils and by the city councils in towns of more than 25,000 inhabitants. As the councils are elected by the taxpayers, both men and women, the members of the first chamber may be regarded as the representatives of the property-owning portion of the community. To be eligible to the first chamber a candidate must be thirty-five years old, own property assessed at $21,000, or pay taxes upon an income of not less than $1,100. Rank does not count. The qualification is pecuniary entirely, and so evenly is property distributed in Sweden that only ten thousand people in the entire kingdom are eligible to the first chamber of the diet.

The members of the second chamber, two hundred and thirty in number, are elected for three years, of whom eighty are elected by the towns and one hundred and fifty by the rural districts. Each must have property worth $270, or have leased $1,600 worth of land for five years, or pay taxes on an income of $214. These are also the qualifications for voting for members of the parliament.

There is very little of politics in Sweden. There are three parties, known as the conservatives, the liberals, and the socialists. The conservative party is comprised of the aristocracy, the church, the agricultural classes and people of conservative sentiment generally. The liberal party is composed of progressive elements, the theorists, the artisans, the machinists, and the thinking men among the laboring element, who advocate a reduction of the tariff on imported merchandise and free trade so far as possible; a separation of church and state on the theory that no man should be taxed to support a religious faith that he does not believe in; a reduction in the army and navy and other official expenses; the modification of the election laws as above stated; rotation in office, so that all shall have a chance, and they oppose the general tendency to centralization in the government.

The socialists go a little farther. They are not so radical as those who go by the same name in Germany, France, and other European countries. They are very moderate in their views. They favor most of the planks in the liberal platform, and, in addition, advocate the adoption of socialistic reforms, the loaning of public money without interest to the poor, public pensions to the helpless, sweeping reforms in the labor laws, and the purchase and maintenance by the state of all public enterprises that affect public welfare, such as the street-car lines, the insurance companies, the banks, etc. The peasants in the country are protectionists and belong to the conservative party. The mechanics in the cities are generally socialists. Politics, however, is not very exciting. The tariff, labor questions, and other propositions are always discussed, and of late years the most interesting issues have been the appropriation of money for national defense, the increase of the term of military service from ninety to three hundred and sixty days for every citizen, the modification of the electoral law, and the regulations of the forests.

Peasants have been members of parliament for more than five hundred years, and now constitute more than half the membership of the second chamber—intelligent, well-educated mechanics and farmers, who take a deep interest in the affairs of the government and generally are on the right side. The agricultural peasants are invariably loyal supporters of the king. The mechanics from the city are usually opposed to him.

The annual session of the riksdag opens immediately after the holidays with a great deal of pomp and ceremony. It is one of the most imposing functions in all Europe. The members of both houses meet at their respective halls, attend divine service at the cathedral, where they receive the sacrament and listen to a sermon of admonition. Then they march in a body to the royal palace, where they are received by the king's ministers with great formality, and escorted to what is known as the throne room. As they enter, each man bows reverently to a silver throne which stands upon a dais at the other end of the apartment. The members of the first chamber are seated on the right side of the great hall, and those of the second upon the left.

When the sound of trumpets is heard, all rise, and the master of ceremonies enters in gorgeous apparel, followed by four pages in dress of the sixteenth century. Behind them is a squad of trumpeters, then the grand marshal of the court, preceded by four heralds and followed by the assistant marshals, the grand chamberlain, the lord steward, the master of the horse, and other officers of the royal household, the eighteen judges of the supreme court, the archbishop and bishops, and the members of the king's cabinet.

Then follows a guard of honor, composed of the highest nobles of the kingdom in glittering uniforms and carrying old-fashioned weapons, such as were once used in actual warfare. They surround the king, who wears his royal robes, and, as he enters, the band plays the favorite air of the people, "From the Depths of the Swedish Heart." He wears the crown of state and a purple robe bordered and lined with crimson the two corners of which are carried by chamberlains Upon the right side of the king walks the prime minister of Sweden. Following the king walk his sons, the princes of the royal house.

When the king has reached the center of the room, he stops, turns with great dignity and bows first to one chamber and then to the other, and then to the queen, who has taken her position in the balcony, attended by the princesses and other members of the royal family and the officers of the court. Then he proceeds slowly until he ascends the dais and seats himself upon the throne, his minister of state occupying a position on his right. Before the separation of the Union, the Norwegian minister of state sat upon his left.

The grand marshal steps forward and strikes the floor three times with a long staff of silver, tipped with jewels. At this signal all arise again except the king. In old-fashioned Swedish the heralds command silence. The king, seated upon his throne, reads his speech, which always begins, "Good gentlemen and Swedish men." The prime minister then reads a review of the acts of state since the adjournment of parliament, which he skims over as rapidly as possible, because the printed copy will be placed in the hands of every person present as soon as the ceremony is over. The presiding officers of the two houses of parliament step forward and make speeches of congratulation, and reassure their sovereign of their loyalty and respect. The king then rises, bows first to the queen, and to each house in turn, and slowly leaves the chamber accompanied by the procession that followed him in.

The courts of Sweden are conducted upon the French plan, and no jury is ever impaneled except in cases concerning the liberty of the press. When a newspaper is accused of libel or sedition, the complainant, whether he be a member of the police or any other official of the government, chooses three jurymen, the defendant three, and the court three. These nine men hear and decide the merits of the case without application of such strict rules of evidence as prevail in the legal practice of the United States. All judicial procedure in Sweden is based upon the assumption that the court is sufficiently intelligent and impartial to determine the reliability of witnesses and to judge of the application of facts laid before it. All judges and judicial magistrates are appointed for life on good behavior, but they can be impeached by processes similar to those authorized by the Constitution of the United States.[g]

CHAPTER VIII
THE ARMY AND NAVY

Everybody in Norway, that is every man, has to serve five years in the army, so that every citizen is a soldier—the first year after the twenty-third birthday seventy days, and thirty days or so each year thereafter for four years more. The organization has a nominal strength of 80,000 men of three divisions known as the landstrom, or reserves (25,000); the landvern, or militia (55,000), and the opbud, or regulars, who numbered about 5,000, garrison the different fortresses along the coast. Every able-bodied Norwegian, except pilots and clergymen, is obliged to serve in any position to which he is assigned by the king, who is commander-in-chief. The sailors and fishermen are enrolled in the navy and must serve aboard a man-of-war at least twelve months. The land forces require five months' service for infantry, seven months for cavalry and artillery, and six months for engineers, which is distributed over a period of five years. Training camps are established every summer in convenient localities from two to three months. Every man capable of bearing arms is in time of war liable to do service in the reserves, from the eighteenth to the fiftieth year of age.

The organization is complete throughout the nation, so that an army of 80,000 men can be mobilized in a few days. Every cavalryman and artilleryman is required to bring a horse with him when he is called to camp, and the arsenals contain a complete equipment of arms and accoutrements. The non-commissioned officers are former members of the regular army, in which they must have served three years in the infantry and cavalry or four years in artillery and engineers. During this period they are given a practical education in books and in the mechanical duties of the soldier. They are taught to repair guns, manufacture powder, make harness, shoe horses, and do everything else that is likely to come within their experience in the field. This training is highly valued by the young men of the country, particularly by boys from the farms, because it gives them a certain social standing, the right to wear a uniform, and a corresponding amount of influence in the community. This regular army school takes in about 1,700 young men every year.

The officers are educated in a military college. The complete course covers five years for the staff, artillery, and engineer corps. Candidates must first have graduated from one of the government technical schools. The infantry and cavalry course is three years. Graduates are appointed second lieutenants in the regular army, and are promoted through the regular grades.

The army of Norway costs the government about 14,000,000 kroner, or $3,800,000 a year, which is an average of $1.70 per capita of the population, or half the tax paid by the English and Germans. The last budget was about $1,000,000 larger than usual, for the purpose of erecting new fortresses upon the southern coast. All the principal seaports are already fortified, and there is an excellent system of torpedo defense in the different fjords, but there is a remarkable public apprehension concerning the intentions of Russia; and, mindful of the fate of Finland, the Norwegians are preparing to resist any aggressiveness on the part of the czar. It is not disputed that Russia desires a winter port on her northern coast for St. Petersburg and Kronstadt are always closed by the ice for five and sometimes six months in the year. The Norwegian fjords never freeze. They are protected by the monstrous mountains, and the water is tempered by warm currents that flow in from the gulf stream. The national apprehension of both Norway and Sweden that Russia covets one of their seaports has existed a good many years. The bugbear has appeared at intervals for half a century, and a great deal of money has been expended in preparations to meet it. The people are, therefore, cordially patriotic in their support of the army, although many of them emigrate to the United States to avoid military service.

Norway has a small but efficient navy, composed of third and fourth class cruisers, monitors, small gunboats and torpedo boats, forty-six in all, aggregating 29,000 tons, 53,000 horse-power, carry 174 guns, and manned by 140 officers and 1,000 men. The officers are educated in naval schools, with a five-year course for regulars and three years for the reserves, which include all the merchant sailors and fishermen.

Norway has taken an active part in the promotion of international arbitration, and has sent delegates to every conference on that subject. The storthing, in a decided manner, has repeatedly expressed its belief in that method of settling disputes, and in correspondence with the Russian government has laid a foundation that may be useful in case the czar, under any pretext, should use aggressive measures in this direction. So much interest has been shown in the question that Alfred Nobel, the Swedish philanthropist, and the inventor of dynamite, who made his money manufacturing that most powerful explosive, by his will authorized the members of the Norwegian storthing to award a prize of $40,000 annually to the person who, in their judgment, during the preceding year, shall have done the most to promote peace among nations and the adoption of the plan of arbitration in the settlement of international differences.

For many years the chief political issue in Sweden has been the increase of the army and the military service required of each citizen. The king finally won, and in 1901 a law was passed increasing the term of service from ninety days to eight and twelve months. The nation claims that period in the life of every able-bodied man, and it is given more or less reluctantly.

Every male citizen is enrolled in the army, and at the time when he becomes twenty-one years of age, he is required to report himself at the military headquarters nearest home, where he submits to a physical examination, and if accepted, is assigned to the proper company and regiment of militia, and directed to report for duty to his immediate commander. The small number of persons rejected for disability is good testimony to the health and vigor of the race. Severe penalties are placed upon those who attempt to escape military service by feigning illness or maiming themselves, but it is said there are still men who would cut off one or two of their fingers and run risk of spending four years in the penetentiary in preference to spending a couple of months every year under military instruction. The military spirit in Sweden is not strong, although history shows that there are no better fighters in the human family, and it is remarkable to watch the high degree of efficiency to which green boys from the farms can be brought after a few weeks of drill and discipline.

The regular army of Sweden oh a peace footing is composed of 34,329 enlisted men, 3,729 officers, 1,655 musicians, 840 engineers, and 623 members of the staff, making a total effective fighting force of 39,114. Of these 6,891 are cavalry and 3,432 artillery.

These forces compose the garrisons at Stockholm and other principal cities of the country, and are at all times under arms. The militia, divided into regiments and companies according to location, numbers 181,000 men, and is subject to call by the king at all hours and under all circumstances. Each member of the militia, as I have said, must serve a certain time in the army, eight months for infantry and twelve months for cavalry and artillery, the service being extended over the period of five years. During this five years a man spends from two to four months each year in a garrison or camp, according to the judgment of his commanding officers, when he receives the nominal pay of the private in the regular army. He has no option as to the time of the annual period or service. He may be asked to remain in the army for eight or twelve months continuously; it all depends upon the plans of the war office.

When a man has served his time in the militia, he is given a certificate to that effect, which exempts him from further active military service, and makes him a member of the reserves, which number 203,000 men, all of whom have served in the militia, and are subject to the summons of the king whenever the country is invaded by foreign foe. With local troubles they have nothing to do. The militia is considered sufficient for any such emergency, but under the Swedish system the effective force at the command of the king in case of foreign invasion is something like 420,000 men.

There are a lot of picturesque old castles and fortresses on the coast of Sweden in which garrisons are still maintained, but they would not last an hour if attacked by modern guns and projectiles. They are reinforced, however, by earthworks, with the very best artillery. Swedish guns rank among the highest, and several Swedish patents in ordnance have been already adopted by the fortification board of the United States. All the harbors are protected by torpedoes, and Stockholm is absolutely impregnable from the sea, being situated upon a fjord or bay that can not be entered except through passages that are easily defended.

The navy of Sweden is comparatively small, but for its numerical strength it is probably the most effective in the world. At least that is the opinion of competent critics. The total force numbers 4,500 officers and men on a peace footing, which may be increased to 8,500 from the reserve on a few hours' notice. The fleet consists of fourteen first-class cruisers and battle ships, four second- and nine third-class, five torpedo catchers, twenty-six torpedo boats, and twenty gunboats of small tonnage, the armament of the fleet being 290 guns and ninety-seven rapid-firing guns. All the vessels were built in Sweden.

Every Swede is a sailor. He is brought up on the water, and taught in childhood to swim and to sail a boat, and, although the shipping industry is not so extensive as in Norway, the national interest in aquatic sports is probably greater and more general than in any other nation. The long line of seacoast and the 1,100 lakes within Swedish territory gives abundant opportunity for the exercise of this inclination. Hence in the case of war, the navy could be recruited indefinitely with competent men.

King Oscar took a deep personal interest in naval affairs, because his early life was spent in the navy, his commission as lieutenant bearing the date of June 19, 1845. When he was called to the throne, he at once commenced to plan for improvement of that branch of the service, and for many years was virtually his own minister of marine. He did much to encourage the maritime spirit among the people, being honorary president of the Royal Yacht Club, and presided over its meetings, which were sometimes held in the palace to suit his convenience. He took an active part in the organization and promotion of the naval reserve, and never lost an opportunity to show his zeal in the development of the shipping industry and the aquatic pastimes.

Nor was the king a paper sailor. On special occasions he showed great bravery and presence of mind at sea, and of his sixty decorations and medals he valued none higher than that which was awarded him by the Humane Society of France in 1862, when he saved the lives of three people at the risk of his own.

The Swedish militia is commanded by officers of the regular army. No man can receive a commission in the militia unless he has spent at least sixteen months in the military academy and passed the required examinations. About a thousand young men are graduated each year from the several schools situated in different parts of the country, which are a part of the regular educational system of the nation. Thus the government has at its command abundant material for the military organization. The officers are promoted as vacancies occur, are retired on half pay when they are aged or disabled—generals at 65 years, colonels at 60, lieutenant colonels and majors at 55, and captains at 50. Militia officers are eligible to appointments in the civil service; they may be elected to the riksdag, and they have the same social standing at the palace as the officers of the regular army. The palace is the center of the social system in Sweden, and only certain persons are eligible to invitations to the king's balls and dinners. All officers of the militia are included in the list, and all peasants in the riksdag, although their wives are never invited.[h]

CHAPTER IX
PUBLIC EDUCATION

There are few countries in which education is as free as in Sweden. From the grammar school to the university in all its stages, the cost is defrayed entirely by the state or the parish. Education is thus not a privilege of the wealthy, but a benefit common to all.

In Norway you are scarcely ever out of sight of a schoolhouse, and Professor Nielsen, of the university, on being asked concerning the ratio of the illiterates, looked surprised and replied that he was not aware of any illiterates; that he did not recollect having seen any statistics on the subject, and ventured to assert that anybody in Norway could both read and write.

Education is free throughout the entire primary system, a course of seven years, between the ages of seven and fourteen, when the law prohibits the employment of children in any occupation, and requires them to attend school at least thirty hours a week for twelve weeks each year in the country and fifteen weeks in the cities. The maximum term is forty weeks in both city and country districts. There are in the kingdom 5,923 school districts, governed by *Skolestyret*—boards consisting of the parish priest, the president of the municipal council, and one of the teachers chosen by themselves. There is also a board of supervisors, composed of three men or women, elected by the parents of the parish. Childless people are not allowed to vote. This board of supervisors does not appear to have any definite function except to advise and find fault. The school board elects the teachers, determines the courses of study and methods of discipline, and submits recommendations and estimates for appropriations annually to the municipal council. In both city and country what is called "voluntary instruction" is provided outside of the legal school hours, which may be taken advantage of by people who are willing to pay for additional attention from the school teachers, but it is neither free nor compulsory.

The compulsory studies in the primary schools are the Bible, the catechism of the Lutheran creed, the Norwegian language, the usual elementary branches, with history (including a treatise on the constitution and the government of Norway), botany, physiology (including the fundamental principles of hygiene and the effects of the use of intoxicating liquors), singing, drawing, wood-carving, the use of the lathe and other tools, manual training, gymnastics, and rifle shooting.

The national law requires that schoolhouses shall be so located as to be within a distance of two miles of the residences of ninety per cent of the children of school age. The poor are provided with text-books upon application, and in some places the municipal council provides every child a warm dinner at noon. It can be paid for if the parents prefer, but the better classes look upon this provision with prejudice, as they do upon all charities. Nevertheless, it is an excellent idea to be sure that the children of the poor get at least one warm meal every day. In the city of Christiania, 711,302 meals are served annually in the primary schools. The average attendance is 22,750, so that only about 24 per cent of the children take advantage of the free dinner. Only 18,341 of these meals are paid for, and those are taken on stormy days by children of well-to-do parents.

The Norway school teachers must be graduates of normal schools, of which there are twelve in the kingdom; they must pass examinations and serve a probation of three months before they are definitely engaged, but when they have once received an appointment, they are settled for life and sure of a pension at the end of the long term of faithful service. The same rule applies to all civil service employees, for the school system is a part of the government. There is no such thing as rotation in office. Promotion is expected by all who deserve it. A worthy and efficient teacher, having begun in youth at the lowest grade, expects advancement to the highest, according to the judgment of the school boards and supervisors. School teaching is a career, just as a government clerkship is a career. People enter both professions with the expectation of making them their life-work, although from our point of view they offer very little inducement.

The average salary of the school teachers in Norway is only about $220 a year, the men receiving a little above the average and the women a little less. The highest salaries are paid in the city of Christiania—$756 for men and $434 for women. Head masters to the number of 1,992, like parsons, are furnished with houses to live in and little tracts of land, three or four acres, where they can raise vegetables for their families and keep cows; and nine hundred and ten of them add a little to their incomes by serving as parish clerks. When they become too old to teach, they receive pensions of from $56 to $224 a year, and when they die, their widows are remembered by the government to the extent of from $28 to $74 per year.

The primary school system of Norway costs an average of $5.60 per child per year in the country, and $13.16 per child in the city, or $1.26 per capita of population in a year.

There is a secondary school system under the control of the national government, administered by the department of education and religion. It embraces forty-six high schools, located in different parts of the country, known as *Latin-Gymnasier*, or classical schools, at which students are prepared for the university, and *Real-Gymnasier*, or technical schools, in which they are taught English, mathematics, the natural and applied sciences, bookkeeping, stenography, and other branches that will fit them for commercial or industrial pursuits. There are also twelve cathedral schools, one for each ecclesiastical diocese, which were founded in the middle ages, and are supported by large estates acquired from the early kings and by confiscation of church property after the Reformation. There are also five private academies, attended chiefly by the sons of rich men.

The University of Christiania, which is one of the first in Europe, was founded in 1811, and has five faculties, with sixty-three professors, eighteen fellows, and about 1,450 students, of whom 70 are studying theology, 20 law, 330 medicine, and 600 are in the scientific department. The professors are appointed by the king, and receive salaries of about $950 a year, with a longevity allowance in addition amounting to about $125 every five years. The fellows are paid about $350 a year, and are provided with lodging rooms. Tuition at the university is free upon payment of a matriculation fee of $10. Women have been admitted on even terms with men since 1882, and 260 have matriculated, of whom 53 have taken degrees. The university has an endowment of $1,310,000, with legacies amounting to about $250,000 to encourage original investigations in special lines of study. The Nansen fund, which amounts to about $150,000, is intended to encourage exploration on the seas. The hospitals of Christiania are in charge of the medical department.

There are also the usual schools for the deaf, dumb, blind, weak-minded, and crippled children, supported by the state, and reform schools for the correction and restraint of the depraved. Technical schools, with day and night classes, for teaching the trades to young men and women, four schools of engineering in different parts of the country, nine industrial schools for women only, where they can be trained to earn their living by sewing, dressmaking, weaving, millinery, embroidery, and other needlework, bookkeeping, typesetting, stenography, typewriting, photography, and other lines of industry, and an art school especially patronized by the king in connection with the art gallery at Christiania, where painting, drawing, and designing, modeling, decoration, and the art of architecture are taught.

In most of the counties are found what are called *Amtsskoler*—schools to educate people for a practical life, with separate courses for each sex, the boys being taught farming, gardening, and mechanics, and the girls the arts of the household. There are also schools of deportment, where girls are fitted to act as governesses and are taught the social graces, music, dancing, the languages, and conversation. In several of the cities are workingmen's colleges, known as *Arbeiderakademier*, where mechanics who have an ambition to acquire a better knowledge of their trades and general culture, may attend lectures in the evenings, delivered by scientific men, successful mechanics, and other specialists. The range of subjects includes every branch of human activity.

In Sweden, in the *Folkskola*, Elementary or People's School, maintained by the parish under the direction of the school board and the close supervision of the state, instruction is compulsory as well as gratuitous. As in Norway, between the ages of seven and fourteen every boy and girl must attend a public school, unless the parents can show that their child is receiving equivalent instruction elsewhere, in a private school or at home. No exception or compromise is allowed, and no "half-time" system or "rush" through the school to suit the convenience of the factory or the farmer. For seven years, during eight and a half months of the year,—allowing for summer, Christmas and Easter holidays,—and thirty-six hours per week, every boy and girl in the kingdom receives instruction and goes through the same curriculum. The school board, which has the direct management of the schools is elected to the parish, and women are eligible to it. The state, which controls the whole system of education, from the A.B.C. class to the college and university, maintains alike its unity and its efficiency, and sees to the strict enforcement of the law. Parents who try to evade it, through malevolence or neglect, may even, after due warning, be deprived of their children, who are taken over by the community during their school years.

In thinly populated districts the school may be "ambulatory," held now in one part of the district and now in another, so that all may attend in turn. In such cases the schooling is reduced to four months in the year. But there is no district, however poor or thinly populated, without its *Folkskola*. There are nearly twelve hundred of these in the land, attended by seven hundred and forty-two thousand pupils, and employing sixteen thousand two hundred and seventy teachers of both sexes.

No more conscientious, hardworking, and respectable class of men and women can be found than the teachers. Eight years' study, first in a special seminary and then in a training college, has taught them their profession both in theory and practice. They are convinced of the importance and dignity of their office, and are respected accordingly. Socially, the general type of the school teacher is a superior one. There are at present in the Riksdag, occupying seats as members of the second chamber, no fewer than eleven teachers in elementary schools, twelve teachers in secondary schools, one inspector of schools, and one university professor. In the rural community, the school teacher is something of an authority. Most of the members of the parish have "sat under him" at school in their early life, and owe to him most of what they know. For years he has been diffusing knowledge around him, and has been looked up to as the fountain of book learning. He is the local parson's great coadjutor in parish matters, and being a ready speaker, is of no mean influence in the parish assemblies. The one dark blot in the existence of the school teacher is the small salary received. Few of them receive so much as $300 a year, the average running from $225 to $275; even in Stockholm the figure going little beyond $300. Living is, however, cheap in the rural districts, and these teachers, who are drawn generally from the rural and indigent classes, are accustomed to frugality and economy. They are lodged free of rent in the schoolhouse or a cottage attached to it, and are allowed firewood and other small prerequisites. They have generally a small garden or potato patch to cultivate, and can keep a cow and a few hens. They often add to their modest stipend by extra work, such as teaching in the evening classes, playing the organ in church, and writing, or some such work after school hours.

At fifteen, after seven years' assiduous attendance at the *Folkskola*, the boy and girl have finished their education, so far as compulsory instruction goes, and they are free to begin work on their father's farm, in his shop or his trade, or take service anywhere and shift for themselves. They may, however, if they like, pursue their studies further in the continuation schools, or in the evening classes provided in most parishes, or repair to a college or gymnasium town, if they elect to enter the church, the liberal professions, or the service of the state. But they have first to be confirmed, and it is here that the definite religious instruction is given. The preparation for confirmation, which entails a much longer and more advanced course of religious instruction than is usual for confirmation in England, is independent of the school and takes place in church, parents being allowed every liberty in the choice of the clergyman who performs this office for their children. English readers who are acquainted with Longfellow's admirable translation of Tegnér's beautiful poem, "The Children of the Lord's Supper," are aware of the importance of this ceremony in Swedish social life. It is the great turning point in the existence of Scandinavian youth. The boy and girl emerging from it leave boyhood and girlhood behind them. Knee-breeches and short frocks have given way to pants and long skirts. The boy sports his first watch and glories in his first shirt-front. The girl discards her long plaits, and wears her hair in a top-knot. They have made their profession of faith in public, have been examined in regard to it, and have had to answer for it in the presence of the whole congregation. They have assumed henceforth the full responsibility of their acts. In the eyes of the church, if not in the eyes of the law, they are free and responsible members of society.

The secondary schools are maintained by the state, and are confined to the towns. They comprise nine forms in seven classes, of which the last two have double forms. The first three correspond to the curriculum of the primary schools, where are taught reading, writing, arithmetic, history, natural sciences, singing, drawing, and gymnastics, to which are added *Sloyd* and gardening for the boys, and needlework and cooking for the girls. Scholars who have passed these in the primary schools enter into the fourth form. They are generally divided into two branches, the classical and the modern, according as the classics or languages predominate in the curriculum, which comprises religion, Swedish composition, history, geography, philosophy, Latin, Greek, German, French, mathematics, zoology, botany, physics, chemistry, and drawing. After the fourth form, pupils must declare, with the written approbation of their parents or guardians, whether they will follow the classical or non-classical course, according as they intend to qualify for the universities or the technical high schools. Not all the pupils who attend these secondary schools complete the full course and pass the final examination. More than half—those who mean to devote themselves to trade, agriculture, or industry, and those who have not developed the capabilities necessary to confront the severe final test of the "maturity" examination—leave the school on attaining the upper forms. To those who intend to enter the professions, the civil and military service, and the church, the full course of the secondary school is necessary, the "maturity" examination certificate being the only open sesame to the universities, the special colleges, and the technical high schools. To obtain it and to don the white cap, which is the outward and visible sign of university membership, is the first great step in the life of the ambitious youth.

For young men destined for the technical trades and professions, there are open, after they have passed the maturity examination at the secondary school, two special institutions, where they complete their technical training—the Technical High School of Stockholm, and the Chalmers Technical Institute at Gothenburg, besides elementary technical schools at other places. The Stockholm Technical School, which is the most complete, comprises five branches: (1) mechanical technology and machinery, shipbuilding and electrotechnics; (2) chemical technology; (3) mineralogy, metallurgy, and mining mechanics; (4) architecture; (5) engineering.

The course in each of these sections takes between three and four years. Generally several are combined, constituting a course of six or seven years.

There are two universities in Sweden—Upsala in the north, founded in 1477; and Lund in the south, founded in 1668, to which may be added the Medical College in Stockholm, founded in 1810, and limited to the medical faculty. The studies at these universities are thorough and comprehensive, but unusually long. They have each four faculties,—theology, jurisprudence, medicine, and philosophy,—and grant three different degrees in each, besides special degrees in theology and jurisprudence for entering the church and the government services. Even these last, which are easiest to obtain, require a course of from four to five years. To take a medical degree a young man must stay nine years at the university, and two additional years in the hospitals, making eleven years in all. Unlike English and American universities, the Swedish universities are non-residential. Like those of the Continent, they are only teaching institutions, and the students who matriculate at Upsala and Lund must lodge in town or board with families living there. Beyond attending the lectures and going up to be tested, they have no direct intercourse with their professors.

In this brief sketch of the institutions provided by the state it will be seen that what especially characterizes public instruction in Norway and Sweden is its undoubted thoroughness and depth, though a serious penalty is paid for this in the extreme length of the course. By the time it is completed, and the young man issues from the protracted ordeal, armed for the battle of life, several of the best years of his youth are passed; he is already between twenty-five and thirty years of age when he first treads on the threshold of his career. On the other hand, he enters it not only with the necessary qualifications whereby to rise to eminence in it, of which the severe tests he has undergone offer evident proof, but with the assurance of finding the way more or less open to success.[i]

CHAPTER X
HAAKON VII, THE NEW KING OF NORWAY

There is something essentially, almost ludicrously, modern about the creation of Norway's new king. Not that it is the first time a sovereign has been, so to speak, "custom-made." An eligible foreign prince is tendered a seat upon an ancient throne; the form is old, but the spirit, how new! Republican though she is to the backbone, Norway has elected to be governed by monarchical methods, fearing with her isolated and primitive peasantry, to put the machinery of control into the hands of the people themselves. She must have a king, but he shall be of a new variety; in short, a republican king. She will not even have him addressed as were the monarchs of old, by the Norwegian equivalent of "Your Majesty." He shall be just *Herre Konge*, plain "Mister the King."

Even as the Norwegians welcomed Haakon VII to their shores, they took pains to show him clearly his rightful place. In his address delivered to the newly arrived sovereign on board the battleship Heimdal, Herr Michelsen, President of Council, and for six months virtual President of Norway, used these significant words: "For nearly six centuries the Norwegian people have had no king of their own. To-day a king of Norway comes to make his home in the Norwegian capital, elected by a free people to occupy, conjointly with free men, the first place in the land. The Norwegian people love their liberty, their independence, and their autonomous government which they themselves have won. It will be the glory of the king and his highest pleasure to protect this sentiment, finding his support in the people themselves. This is why the Norwegian people hail you to-day with profound joy and cry, 'Long live the King and Queen of Norway!'"

Was ever so frank a bargain driven with a king before? "Behold," says Norway in effect, "you may sit on a throne; but beware how you attempt to king it over us. We will give you a salary to transact our official business and act as official figurehead. But you must never overlook the fact that it was we who made you and not you yourself."

Is it any wonder that when asked to undertake to govern a people so independent, so proud spirited as this, Prince Karl of Denmark took time to think? Or that he asked for a popular vote that he might know how large a proportion of the *frei* people of Norway really wanted him for a king?

This was not the only reason why he hesitated. Being himself on his mother's side a Bernadotte, he could scarcely ascend the Norwegian throne without the friendly sanction of Sweden. Moreover, his wife, Princess Maud of England, was more than reluctant to undertake life in Christiania and the duties of queenship. Lastly, Prince Charles himself ran a shrewd risk in assuming the crown, lest, should his relations with Norway become difficult, he might be forced to resign, and find himself—having abandoned his naval career for the throne—in a state of abject poverty.

All three objections were finally overruled. Sweden, fearing lest an empty throne in Norway should give impetus to the movement for a republic, and that such a movement might afterward spread to her own borders, was as much in haste to see Norwegian affairs settled as the Norwegians themselves, so she swallowed her grievances. Most amicable correspondence passed between Prince Karl and the Crown Prince of Sweden, the latter expressing himself anxious to be the first to welcome Haakon VII into his capital. What became of Princess Maud's reluctance is not definitely known. It is understood that she never found life at the Danish court very amusing, and probably the prospect of exchanging Copenhagen for a city of less than half its size did not allure her. She must have realized that if she accepted a share of the Norwegian throne, she would be forced to abandon her favorite cure for *ennui*—frequent flights to the court of England—for Norway has had quite enough of absentee royalty. The English papers asserted that King Edward used his parental authority to overcome his daughter's scruples. At all events, she gave in. As for Prince Karl's reasonable fear of dethronement and penury, the Norwegian government quieted that by promising a respectable pension in case the king should find it expedient to abdicate.

So, then, the affair was comfortably arranged. The king has a salary of $200,000, a crown when he had no hope of ever feeling one on his brow, and the problems of a court without a nobility.

And now the world is asking, "Has Norway done well for herself?" Certainly she has done well in putting a Scandinavian prince on the throne. No alien would ever understand Norway or be understood. If reports are creditable, the Kaiser made the most of his friendship with the country in support of the claims of a son of his own. Had a German secured the throne, there would have been sown fresh seeds of discord on a peninsula which can raise a sufficient crop of dissensions without any aid from the rest of Europe. For Denmark, still nursing the rankling grievance of the Schleswig-Holstein affair, detests the thought of everything German.

King Haakon combines the advantages of Scandinavian birth with the very positive political asset of blood relationship to half the courts of Europe. Grandson of the late King Christian of Denmark, the young monarch is also nephew to King George of Greece, the Dowager Empress of Russia, and Alexandria of England, a grand-nephew to the late Oscar of Sweden, son-in-law to King Edward VII, and cousin to the Czar. To a relatively defenseless country like Norway, this means a good deal.

In himself the new king is a clean-lived, healthy young man of thirty-three, in personality quite fit to represent a nation which thinks well of itself. Tall, though not quite so tall as his uncle, Prince Christian, whose mark on the famous old royal measuring-column at Roskilde comes just under that of the giant, Peter the Great, King Haakon is slight, yet vigorous-looking, and splendidly well set up. The face, while scarcely so handsome as the profile pictures lead us to think, is a distinguished one, and has for Norway this charm, that it is markedly not of the Bernadotte type, although his mother is a Bernadotte. Those who know him describe him as an extremely intelligent and sensible young man, easy and tolerant without being weak, and capable of strenuous devotion to hard work. These things bespeak an industrious, efficient, and tractable king, such as the Norwegians, who would equally resent either vacillation or tyranny, know how to appreciate.

It has been said in France that King Haakon abandons tiller and compass for crown and scepter without one hour's training in politics or diplomacy.

The statement appears incontestable. In view of the remarkable longevity of the late king of Denmark, and the excellent health and prospects of the Crown Prince and his immediate heir, this younger son of a royal house was not brought up to look for a crown. Instead, he was destined from the outset for a naval career. For all that, it is not safe to say that he has had no training in politics or diplomacy. One can scarcely grow up in the family of the "father-in-law of Europe" and not learn the principles of the great game of world affairs. King Haakon is no stranger to the queer old palace among the beeches at Fredensborg, where every summer King Christian gathered together his children and grandchildren and great-grandchildren from the courts of England, Russia, Denmark, Sweden, and Greece; and where conversations took place which, if reported, would vitally interest the whole round world. In his lifetime, the Czar Alexander III was particularly fond of holding long talks at Fredensborg with his nephew Karl, then a lieutenant of the navy, whom he found especially intelligent and open-minded.

It is thought in Copenhagen that King Haakon may, even during the last years of his father's life, have had some experience in the government of Denmark, since his father, the Crown Prince, was called upon to perform many of the old king's duties. At least, if he did not actually transact royal business, he acquired no small acquaintance with the working of government machinery.

Nothing, certainly, could have been more fitting than that a ruler of Vikingland should be educated for the sea. Nor could anything have been devised better calculated to knock the nonsense out of a princeling than apprenticeship in the Danish navy. Hrolf Wisby, who messed with Prince Karl when he was a naval cadet, says that the lad was at first little more than a piece of court furniture. Any one who is familiar with the appalling frankness and unvarnished brusquerie of grown-up Danes can judge whether the hazing and horse-play on a Danish man-of-war was agreeable, and whether it was medicinal in a case of congenital self-esteem. Prince Karl lived the life of an ordinary middy, scrubbed decks, mended his own clothes, slept in a hammock, and ate provender which was anything but fit to set before a king. It is recorded of him that he was an expert in polishing a certain brass binnacle lantern. We wonder if he ever thinks now of a certain line in Pinafore, "I polished that handle so care-ful-lee, that now —"

As ensign, second lieutenant, first lieutenant, and finally captain of a frigate, the young man acquitted himself well, earning the reputation of a capital officer, hardworking, careful, no martinet towards his men, though by no means to be trifled with. In practical seamanship, he excels any other prince of his age, and can command any kind of naval craft from torpedo boat to battleship, and lead in actual battle.

In forming their court, King Haakon and Queen Maud are gathering about them the literary, artistic, and musical people of the realm, for they are devoted to the companionship of gifted folk. The queen has herself written plays under the pseudonym "Graham Irving," and the king paints a little in aquarelles, and plays the piano almost too well to be termed an amateur. Both are accomplished linguists, speaking with discrimination French, German, Russian, English, Norwegian, Swedish, and, naturally, Danish. There is no barrier of speech in their intercourse with members of the diplomatic corps.

The little heir apparent, Alexander, rechristened Olaf, has already done much toward ingratiating himself with the Norwegian people, although but a half dozen years old. On the day when the royal couple entered Christiania, the boy was but two and a half years old, but he was very much interested in the decorations, and seemed to catch the enthusiasm of the crowd, for he waved his little hand spontaneously. In counting up the merits of the king, the promising little heir must by no means be left out.

Trondhjem Cathedral, where all the kings and queens of Norway for centuries have been crowned, and where the coronation of King Haakon VII and Queen Maud occurred, stands on the site of what was undoubtedly the first Christian church in the country—that erected by Olaf Trygvason in 996. Within its confines bubbles the spring which sprang from the tomb of that later Olaf who is the patron saint of Norway, and somewhere under its walls lie moldering the bones of medieval kings, four of whom accepted their consecration before the altar where King Haakon received his crown. It is a thousand pities that hammer and chisel should have exorcised the spirits which ought to haunt this venerable shrine. It is as if England's Abbey had been scrubbed and resurfaced, and new noses had been provided for all the crumbling stone kings and queens. Trondhjem Cathedral has burned down so many times, and the work of restoration has been so sweeping, that it takes an active imagination to invest it with the proper glamour of romance.

Trondhjem itself is an odd place for festivities. The people say that it is fear of fire which makes them separate their insignificant wooden houses by such disproportionately broad streets. Certainly it gives to the town a low look anything but imposing.

Whatever may be the esthetic shortcomings of King Haakon's coronation city, it was amply atoned for by the enthusiasm and whole-hearted devotion of his new people. The king and queen are in very truth "the father and mother of the land." Even toward the rulers they shared with Sweden their cherished warm affection until their grievances waxed too sore. When Sophie of Nassau was on her way to Trondhjem to be crowned, in 1873, she drove herself in a carriole from the Romsdal, stopping perforce at humble posting-stations by the way. And everywhere the peasants came with flowers, greeting their queen by the affectionate and familiar "Du." More than once when the press was thick about her, and those on the outskirts could not see, the queen was urged to mount upon the housetop that the eyes of all might be gladdened by the sight of the dear land-mother. There was a significant demonstration of this sort of heart-loyalty when Haakon VII and Queen Maud entered Christiania. The crowds which waited in the steadily falling snow, and shouted themselves hoarse, might be accounted for by curiosity and mob enthusiasm.

Triumphal arches, flags, and even the rain of flowers which descended on the royal pair, might be classed as perfunctory, an essential part of the occasion. But at night the spirit of the people showed beyond mistake. Not only were the streets arched and bordered with festoons of colored incandescent lights, not only were the battleships in the harbor strung with fiery beads to the topmost spar, but every window in every house in the city bore its light. Fine houses had candelabra behind the glass, and the poorest mere tapers, but everywhere the same fire of welcome burned.

Haakon VII has the privilege of ruling over the most united people on the face of the earth. Before the plebiscite, Sweden declared that the desire for separation was confined to a party who were poisoning the minds of the common people. When the plebiscite had shown that only 164 men out of 368,000 could be found to uphold the union, Sweden protested that the peasants had been intimidated and dared not vote as they thought!

Now, it was just at this stirring time that I was driving through Norway, or cruising in her fjords, and talking with graduates of her university, with sea-captains, hotel proprietors, traveling men, porters, drivers, serving-maids—all, in short, who spoke English enough to make themselves clear. It was as if all Norway spoke with one voice. From Hamerfest to Stavanger there was the same complaint of the same wrongs, the same quiet insistence upon the same remedy. Nor was it only the subjects of King Oscar who spoke; Norwegians settled in France, in England, or in America either hurried home to vote or sent their vigorous endorsement of the revolutionary proceedings. A window in Christiania was completely filled by the mingled flags of Norway and the United States, crossed by a banner bearing the words, "For Disunion." It was the voice of Norway and America. It was a modest desire they expressed. In the words of Olaf Sprachehaug, our humble-minded *skydsgut*, the whole country was saying, "And now I t'ink we get a king of our own." They have their own king now, and all the world wishes them joy in him.[j]

CHAPTER XI
THE ROYAL FAMILY OF SWEDEN

The present reigning family of Sweden is too young to be very numerous, and in this brief survey it is well to begin with a bit of information about that grand democratic monarch, Oscar II, passed away less than two years ago. How the Bernadotte dynasty was formed has already been shown in a previous chapter, and something of the kings, who succeeded the former Field Marshal of France has also been related, so that we have in these few pages simply to deal with Oscar II, the late king, and his four sons and their families.

Oscar's grandfather, the originator of the Bernadotte dynasty, was still on the throne when he was born, in 1829, as the third son of Crown Prince Oscar and the beautiful Josephine of Leuchtenberg. He seemed far removed from the throne then, and thus he found freedom to develop himself more in keeping with his individual tastes and inclinations. Another factor to be borne in mind is the character of his governor and principal instructor, the historian, F.F. Carlson, who gave to his pupil a fondness for scientific exactness as well as an insight into the true causes of civilizatory development found none too frequently in professional thinkers, and hardly ever in princes. The things that drew him most strongly in those days were the sea, and music.

One of the foremost of Swedish composers, A.F. Lindblad, taught him the latter, while his fondness for the former was richly satisfied during the years when he worked his way through the ranks of the Swedish navy. And his position on board the various man-of-war's-men in which he traveled on many seas was never merely ornamental or even exceptional. He took not only the title but also the work of the offices he held, from midshipman to admiral.

It was characteristic of him, too, that when he married, he did so out of love. On a tour through several countries; in 1856, he was fortunate enough to meet Princess Sophia of Nassau. The courtship was brief and ardent. Within a few months occurred the engagement, and the wedding followed in less than a year. To the last that royal couple remained strongly devoted to each other in spite of widely differing tastes and temperaments. She has all her life been intensely religious, with a strong leaning toward pietism, and illness has still further developed this inborn tendency. He, on the other hand, was always gay, light-hearted, fond of merriment, and given to many pleasures and pursuits which his spouse could only look upon as far too worldly.

Duke Oscar Frederick, as he was known in those early days, found himself heir to the throne after death had unexpectedly removed the two claimants with rights prior to his own. And on the succession of his eldest brother, he became the Crown Prince. It was a delicate position which imposed on him a reserve foreign to his nature. As it contrasted sharply with the unceremonious jollity of his brother, King Charles, he came by degrees to be regarded by those ignorant of his true character with a distrust bordering on dislike. Thus, when the succession fell to him in 1872, he found himself little understood and less loved. It took him years to overcome the prejudice. Perhaps it was his sanction of the impeachment proceedings by the Norwegian Radicals against the retiring Conservative ministry which, in the early '80's, first served to turn the trend of public opinion in his favor, both in Sweden and Norway. That act was one of the many by which he showed his ability to submit his own inclinations to the demands of the people without becoming a mere tool in the hands of any one political party. About the same time he succeeded in bringing about a deeply needed and by himself long-cherished reform of the popular educational system in Sweden. Previously,—it was, in fact, his first important step after his ascension to the throne,—he had on his own initiative proclaimed full freedom of worship for persons not belonging to the established church.

A Scandinavianism of the purely sentimental kind,—the kind that talked without ever dreaming of putting the talk into deeds,—had prevailed until then on the peninsula. Intermixed with it was an equally sentimental sympathy with France. Though himself the grandson of a Frenchman and still keenly devoted to French literature and art, King Oscar had the foresightedness to recognize that the interests of the country were more closely bound up with those of Germany. And one of the most striking features of his reign was the growing cultural intercourse between the nations in the north and their neighbor south of the Baltic. And while the king discouraged the speech-making, empty Scandinavianism against which Ibsen was fond of launching his most vitriolic invectives, he fostered instead a fellow-feeling between Sweden, Norway and Denmark that found its expression in practical co-operation, in the equalization of commercial and industrial regulations, in the breaking down of as many as possible of the unnecessary barriers between them. As the years passed on and the trend of his labors became understood and appreciated, he found a part of his reward in a steadily increasing respect for him throughout the civilized world, a respect that repeatedly found expression in requests that he act as arbiter of international differences. He had always been fond of traveling, and this fondness he continued to indulge up to the last. Unlike those of some other monarchs having a similar taste, his comings and goings on the Continent were always the objects of pleasant and welcoming comment. If gossip had to name King Christian of Denmark "the father-in-law of all Europe," King Oscar was surely "the friend of all the world." Apace with his own fame grew the prosperity of his people. On either side of the Kjölen his reign marked an era of unprecedented economical, social, and spiritual progress which not even the internal dissensions of the sister nation could interrupt.

King Oscar's motto was *Brödrafolkens Väl* "The Brother-Peoples Weal!" The Scandinavian peninsula is still populated by brother-peoples, as was indicated at the time of the death of the old king. It was the week for the distribution in Norway of the Nobel prizes, always attended in Christiania with great rejoicing and merry-making. On this occasion all demonstration was prohibited, and the Norwegian capital was almost as much in mourning as was Stockholm. Though entirely devoted to the new order of things, the Norwegians did not forget, nor will they forget, the character of the king who ruled them for a generation. More democratic than the Swedes, they were peculiarly attached personally, if not politically, to one whom they felt to be really of like democratic instincts with themselves, even if he did show himself every inch a king.

Not only as a ruler, but as a father, King Oscar was both wise and fortunate. Four sons came to him through his marriage, and these have proved men of his own type. The Crown Prince Gustave was born just one year after the marriage of his parents, on June 16th, at the Castle of Drottingholm, in the year 1858; Prince Oscar, known as Prince Bernadotte, was born on Nov. 15, 1859, at Stockholm; Prince Carl on Feb. 27, 1861, also at Stockholm; while the youngest, Prince Eugene, like his eldest brother, first saw the light at the Castle of Drottingholm, on Aug. 1, 1865. As has been previously stated, the Crown Prince (now king) was married to the Princess Victoria of Bade, granddaughter of Emperor William I of Germany, and great-granddaughter of the exiled Gustavus IV of Sweden. The third son, Prince Carl, is wedded to his cousin, the Princess Ingeborg of Denmark, which was a source of great satisfaction to King Oscar and Queen Sophie. The youngest son, Prince Eugene, is devoted to art, and spends much time out of the country. Never did King Oscar do more to win the approval of his subjects, and thinking men and women everywhere, than when he permitted the marriage of his second son, Prince Oscar, to a young Swedish noblewoman, Fröken Ebba Munck, of Fulkila, who was also Queen Sophie's maid-of-honor. While the prince had to renounce his right of succession and his position as a royal prince of Sweden, his relations to his father and the other members of the royal family remained the same.

Of this incident in the history of the royal family of Sweden, the following story is told:

The Queen interceded long and persistently with her husband for permission for her second son to be married to the woman he loved. Although the Munck family had played a very important part in the history of the nation, the king was opposed to the *mésalliance*. "It is Oscar's duty to be true to himself and to his love," she used to say. But the king, who was not wont to refuse any of the wishes of his consort, steadily refused to sanction the union. There were many things against such a marriage, for Prince Oscar was the second son of the king, and the very fact that the reigning House of Norway and Sweden was one of the most youthful of the royal houses of Europe made it all the more necessary that its scions should intermarry with the members of the ancient reigning houses.

About this time the queen was seized with one of her serious attacks of illness, and her state was such that at one time her life was despaired of. Her physicians declared that her only hope of recovery lay in an instant operation, which was both dangerous and extremely painful.

The queen called the king to her bedside, and said, "If I undergo this operation and recover, will you allow Oscar and Ebba to have their way?" The king was unable to resist such an appeal, made at such a time, and gave his promise. A short time afterwards the operation was successfully performed, and when the queen was convalescent, the king redeemed his promise and gave his consent to the marriage of his second son. It was on Christmas Eve, and the king had come to his wife's apartments to see her. He found Ebba Munck and his son Oscar with her. The maid-of-honor was, at the time of his entrance, singing one of his poems to Her Majesty, which, oddly enough, was on the subject of the right to love. After waiting until the song was ended, the king went up to his son, and, leading him to the girl, laid his hand in hers, in this manner signifying that he had withdrawn his opposition to their plans.

The marriage has proved a most happy one. Prince Oscar has found perfect content, and has been able to follow his career as a philanthropist. The wedding took place at Bournemouth, in the presence of the queen of Sweden, on March 15, 1888, and for some time after it the prince and his wife were known as Prince and Princess Bernadotte; but later the uncle of

Prince Oscar, the Grand Duke of Luxemburg, gave him the title of the Count of Wisborg for himself and his descendants. When their children were born, Prince Oscar and his wife proclaimed them as the children of Oscar and Ebba Bernadotte, and, during their entire married life, they have lived as quietly and simply as possible, and have found their greatest interest in working for the poor and suffering. They have a son and a daughter, the former, Count Carl Oscar, having been born on May 27, 1890, and the latter, the Countess Marie, on February 28, 1889; and three other children.

And so, as the years went by, a third generation grew up in the palace at Stockholm,—a brood of long-limbed and broad-shouldered sons with wholesome tastes and bright minds and kindly temperaments. And at last, when the king was seventy-eight years old, a great-grandchild was laid in his arms,—the first son of Prince Gustavus Adolphus (now the Crown Prince) and the Princess Margaret of Connaught.

Up to the last King Oscar remained active and interested in all public affairs. Though he had experienced several brief but rather severe illnesses of late years, the end came without warning, after a few days of indisposition, on Dec. 8, 1907. A kindly "thanks" for a small favor rendered him by a member of his family was the last word heard from his lips. Previously he had expressed his wish to the members of his cabinet that no interruption in public or private business be made on account of his death.

King Gustavus V, who took the oath of office within a few hours of his father's death, has suffered something resembling his father's fate as Crown Prince. Overshadowed by the more brilliant gifts and more attractive personality of the parent, he was for years spoken of in rather a disparaging manner in Sweden, while in Norway he harvested outright hatred in return for his determined upholding of the union. On frequent occasions during the last decade of his father's reign, he acted as vice-regent while his father was sick or traveling, and in this way he found chances to display qualities that gradually changed the popular regard of him from one of suspicion to one of hearty respect. His near-sightedness, his serious-mindedness, have militated against him, but it seems probable that he will prove the very *best* ruler Sweden could desire at the present juncture. He is slow to make up his mind, and will not do so until he has searched every phase and detail of the problem before him, but once he has come to a conclusion, he pursues his path without looking to the right or left.

Gustavus is fifty years old, tall, rather dark, quite unassuming, and is essentially democratic, while seeming the opposite, whereas Oscar was aristocratic, although he made much of the people. Like all other Swedish kings, Gustavus adopted a motto when he ascended the throne; it is "With the People for the Fatherland" —not inappropriate in view of his inheritance of a problem clamoring for solution, the extension of the suffrage and a more direct representation of the people in both the upper and lower houses of the Riksdag. The new king, who possesses an uncommon amount of energy, may probably be depended upon to accomplish this reform.

There is neither pride of an objectionable type, nor any tendency to tyranny, nor one strain of arrogance in the new king. He may not be able to draw upon such ripe culture or upon such fine talents as the monarch who preceded him, yet the Swedes have no fear that his love of truth and justice will not outweigh this deficiency and probably make him a more practical ruler. As for the French descent of the Swedish royal house, neither the present nor the late king have ever been ashamed of their ancestry, or forgotten that the first Bernadotte on their throne was one of Napoleon's greatest marshals.

Never will Gustavus V be able to give to words or actions that brilliantly original and kingly tone for which his late father was so admired everywhere. That, to the mind of all beholders, is to be the drawback of his reign, for he is the merest mortal; where his father was the luminous angel. Where Oscar would have been finely eloquent, Gustavus shows himself merely sensible. Oscar's temper was heated, his emotions were forever coming to the surface. Gustave is, if more poised, less interesting. He has always been addicted to manly sports and exercises. He has often been observed to "put up" an excellent game of tennis at the club in Stockholm. But he is without the alert and springy step of the old Oscar, whose muscles remained taut and elastic almost to his dying day. Gustave lacks the literary aptitudes of his late father, likewise, who left a well-filled book of verse which admirers all over Europe did into French, German, Italian, Danish, and even Hungarian. Gustave has not inherited his mother's musical genius, either. She was at one time a devotee of Wagner, a disciple of Kant, and always a pious evangelical of the German cast. From both his parents Gustave received every encouragement to proficiency in music. Music, to the late Oscar, was, both in theory and practice, an essential element in the intellectual life. Gustave is less the artist than the practical king.

He encourages international congresses of every kind to come to Sweden; he helps the universities and the cause of education throughout his kingdom; he feels his father's interest in Hedin's travels through central Asia, but he can give no creative impulse after his father's grand fashion. Oscar was the man of ideas, the vitalizer of projects literary, musical, dramatic and scientific. He made Stockholm the capital of the whole intellectual world. Gustave is very courteous, affable in a dignified way, impressive as he opens the Riksdag in royal ermine. He has commenced his reign in simplicity, rising at eight, breakfasting on coffee and rolls, reading the morning papers until ten, and reviewing the military with a conscientious assiduity. His note is repose both in manner and in speech, in striking contrast with the late Oscar, who was majestic in the very way he had of eating cold meat at supper, and whose height of six feet three towered, almost without the drooping heaviness of age, till his seventy-ninth year. Notwithstanding the adverse comparison with his parent, one has but to see Gustave's face, with its determination and refinement, to feel a certain assurance as to Sweden's future.

It is a curious fact that there has been such a dearth of girls in the Swedish royal family, the only princess of the house being the Crown Princess of Denmark, a daughter of the late King Charles XV. The present queen has only sons: Crown Prince Gustavus Adolphus, wedded to Margaret of Connaught; Prince Wilhelm, who was recently married to the Russian Princess Marie Palvona, and Prince Erik, now about twenty years of age. The present Crown Prince and Princess are seemingly perpetuating the tradition, as their first child is a lusty little son.

Queen Victoria is said to be endowed with an instinct for business of every kind far finer and more efficient than that of her husband, and it is to be regretted that her health is so frail that she is obliged to spend much time outside her husband's realm, and the duties of her royal dignity devolve upon her daughter-in-law, the Crown Princess. It is very satisfying to the Swedish people that by a strange play of circumstances, the claims of the extinct House of Vasa,—the last direct descendant of which passed away a few days after King Oscar, in the person of Carola, Dowager-Queen of Saxony, and daughter of the deposed King Gustavus Adolphus IV of Sweden,—are again restored, and that the reigning House of Bernadotte and the ancient House of Vasa have become joined through the present Crown Prince. It is something to consider, too, that Adolphus V is the first of the Bernadotte dynasty in whose veins, through his mother, Sophie of Nassau, there flows royal blood.[k]

CHAPTER XII
CHARITABLE AND BENEVOLENT INSTITUTIONS

This is the age of munificent benefactions in aid of science and learning. The Rhodes scholarships, Mr. Carnegie's free libraries and educational endowments, the Duc d'Aumale's gift to the French Academy of his fine *chatteau* at Chantilly, with its magnificent historical and art collections; many institutions founded in the United States and elsewhere by multi-millionaires for the advancement of knowledge, are a sign of the times. They foreshadow the abolishment of pauperism and its attendant charities to give place to beneficent institutions, and Norway and Sweden are abreast with other countries in this movement. Apart from charitable institutions and endowments for the maintenance of hospitals and asylums, of universities, scholarships and fellowships, which the generosity of former generations has secured, the present generation has seen noble donations made by private men for more special objects, having the general advancement of knowledge in view, such as the encouragement of scientific research and the support of voyages of geographical exploration. Nordenskiöld's Arctic voyages, his and Palander's navigation through the polar northeast passage in the *Vega*, Nathort's exploration of King Carl's Land, the Swedish expedition to the Antarctic regions under Otto Nordenskiöld, which has lately returned after two years' adventurous exploration in Graham Land and the discovery of King Oscar Land, Sven Hedin's travels in Central Asia, which have had such important results and made his works so widely read—all these were undertaken as the result of such aid. The latest case in point, Alfred Nobel's foundation of annual prizes for the reward of scientific discovery, of literary merit, and humanitarian endeavor, deserves special notice. The annual distribution of these prizes, each of which represents a small fortune ($41,500), has of late years fixed the attention of the learned world on the Swedish literary and scientific bodies, and the Norwegian Parliamentary Committee, who were entrusted by him with the difficult and invidious task of awarding them.

Alfred Nobel, the dynamite king, as he was styled, belonged to a family of inventors and industrial magnates. His father, Emmanuel Nobel, was the inventor of nitroglycerine, and of fixed submarine torpedoes or mines. His two brothers, Robert and Louis Nobel, founded the naptha and petroleum works at Bacou, one of the largest industrial enterprises of Russia. Alfred himself invented dynamite and dynamite gum, and a smokeless powder, ballistite, which he patented in 1867, 1876, and 1889. It is mainly due to the works of the Nobel family that Sweden has attained the reputation of Master Producer of Explosives. Chemical research has always been a specialty among Swedish men of science, and a large number of the known chemical elements were discovered and made known by Swedish scientists.

In 1876, Alfred Nobel had perfected his invention of dynamite gum. He went to Paris with his patented invention, and there formed a company with a capital of ten million francs for the manufacture of dynamite. It proved to be an article of the greatest industrial importance, and one destined to revolutionize mining and engineering. Erelong he had established extensive works in France, Scotland, Germany, Belgium, Austria, and the United States. He produced over $25,000,000 worth a year. He became, in fact, the world's purveyor of an article which was now exclusively used in mining and engineering works. Thanks to it, engineers were able to pierce tunnels through the Alps, miners to sink their shafts into the bowels of the earth, and harbor constructors to remove sunken rocks out of the way of shipping. But thanks to it, too, the Communards were enabled to blow up the finest monuments of Paris in a few hours. It was at once a powerful instrument of industrial development, and of progress in the conquest of man over inert matter, and a terrible engine of devastation in warfare, and of massacre and vandalism where homicidal and destructive passions were aroused in mankind.

It was perhaps this thought, that in benefiting industry he had also made war more destructive, which led Alfred Nobel, who was a most pacific and humane man, endowed with the kindliness and sympathy of a great mind, to make the provisions he did in his will. He devoted all his fortune to the encouragement of scientific discovery and the reward of endeavors to diminish standing armies and the chances of war, to promote fraternity among nations, and the settlement of international disputes by peace congresses. His will, in its very conciseness and unsophisticated simplicity, is characteristic of the man. It is dated Nov. 27, 1895, and he died a year afterwards, on Dec. 10, 1896, leaving a fortune of $10,000,000. After instituting several small legacies, the will proceeds:

"With the residue of my convertible estate I hereby direct my executors to proceed as follows: They shall convert my said residue of property into money, which they shall then invest in safe securities; the capital thus secured shall constitute a fund, the interest accruing from which shall be annually awarded in prizes to those persons who shall have contributed most materially to benefit mankind during the year immediately preceding. The said interest shall be divided into five equal amounts, to be apportioned as follows: one share to the person who shall have made the most important discovery or invention in the domain of physics; one share to the person who shall have made the most important chemical discovery or improvement; one share to the person who shall have made the most important discovery in the domain of physiology or medicine; one share to the person who shall have produced in the field of literature the most distinguished work of an idealistic tendency; and, finally, one share to the person who shall have most or best promoted the fraternity of nations and the abolition or diminution of standing armies and the formation or increase of peace congresses. The prizes for physics and chemistry shall be awarded by the Swedish Academy of Science in Stockholm, the one for physiology or medicine by the Caroline Medical Institute in Stockholm; the prize for literature by the Swedish Academy in Stockholm, and that for peace by a committee of five persons to be elected by the Norwegian Storthing. I declare it to be my express desire that, in awarding these prizes, no consideration whatever be paid to the nationality of the candidates, that is to say, the most deserving be awarded the prize, whether of Scandinavian origin or not."

It was Nobel's object to reward and help the pure man of science, too much absorbed in his researches to think of drawing any industrial or pecuniary advantages from his scientific discoveries. "I would not leave anything to a man of action or industrial enterprise," he said to a friend with whom he was discussing the project of his will; "the sudden acquisition of a fortune would probably only damp the energy and weaken the spirit of enterprise of such a man. I want to aid the dreamer, the scientific enthusiast, who forgets everything in the pursuit of his ideas."

It seems like dropping from the sublime to the ridiculous to follow so ideal a benefaction with a report of so mundane a thing as a soup kitchen, but soup is as necessary to humanity at the present period of life as some of the exalted things of the intellect, and, as pauperism in Norway and Sweden is so almost unobservable, it is difficult to search out with the keenest vision any charity that is doing more than are the "steam kitchens" of Norway and Sweden. And the keenest vision would hardly observe that these "steam kitchens" are charitable institutions. They are called "steam kitchens" because they are the first institutions in the peninsula where steam was used for the cooking of food. The one at Stockholm, instituted by Prince Carl, is very similar in detail and operation to the one in Christiania, but the latter was established first and is more perfect in its arrangement and methods, so we will take it for illustration.

This kitchen at Christiania was established in 1858 by benevolent people to provide wholesome food for the poor at low prices. The charter granted to the company limited its profits to six per cent of the capital invested, with a provision that the balance, if any, should be paid into the poor fund of the city. There was a hard struggle at first to make both ends meet, and an annual deficit for many years, which was made up by the stockholders, but at last the "kitchen" became so popular that it began to pay dividends, and the stock has since been watered four times, until it now pays what is equivalent to twenty-four per cent annually upon the original investment, with a surplus larger than the capital on which it was started. It is one of the most profitable enterprises in Europe for the amount of money involved, but that fact does not diminish the benefits conferred upon the public, and the generosity of the company to the poor, particularly in times of labor troubles and financial depression, can not be questioned. Hundreds of bachelors and single women take their meals there regularly, and hundreds of families obtain their entire supply of food, wholesome and well cooked, at nominal cost.

There is a long official title to the company, but nobody ever mentions it. It occupies a two-story building covering nearly half an ordinary block. The location is convenient to the business portion of the city, the docks and the market-place. There are two large halls, one above the other, containing five long tables, seating thirty persons each, thus accommodating three hundred customers at a sitting. In the upstairs room it costs eleven cents in our money for a good dinner; in the lower room it costs nine cents. There are no tablecloths and no napkins, but the tops of the tables have been scoured until they shine and everything is spotless. The whole institution is a model of neatness. It seems remarkable how it can be kept so clean with so many unwashed customers and so much business. The windows are large and let in plenty of light. The walls are covered with bright tints, and the waitresses wear white caps, aprons, and oversleeves. At each place is a knife, fork, spoon, drinking glass, cup and saucer, and a piece of bread about three inches square. Dinner is served from ten in the morning until six in the afternoon to an average of 2,500 people daily. Some of them come twice. They take a cup of coffee and eat a piece of cheese and bread at their homes early in the morning. Then at ten or eleven, and again at four or five o'clock, they go to the "kitchen" for a square meal. Thus it costs them not more than twenty-five cents a day, all told, for their food. In the last ten years they have never served less than 1,500 people in a day.

The bill of fare varies from day to day, but we will take one day, Tuesday, for example. A large dish of barley soup is served, wholesome and nourishing, a ball of hashed meat, with potatoes and rice, or boiled salmon, potatoes and turnips.

The nine-cent dinner is pretty much the same, with the exception of the soup; boiled potatoes and rice, or boiled salmon, potatoes and turnips. A plate of soup alone, which in itself would be more than a meal for most people, being filled with meat and vegetables, is served for three cents.

The same dinners are furnished to the public to be eaten at their homes for nine and seven cents respectively, and usually contain enough food for two or three women, although Norwegians have stalwart appetites. The outdoor service is conducted in another part of the building, upon another street. The patrons procure tickets at an office and then form in line—men, women and children, each with a bucket or a basket, or both, in hand. Many tickets are given gratuitously, but it is impossible to distinguish the paying from the charity customers. Benevolent people throughout the city purchase bunches of tickets, which they give to the poor, and sometimes in lieu of wages. If you hire a man to clean up the yard, you can give him so much cash and so many meal tickets, or if a person appeals to you for relief, it is always better to give a ticket to the "Steam Kitchen" rather than money. Many customers buy two portions which they take home and warm up at meal time for the whole family.

In the center of a large room are rows of immense caldrons with coils of steam pipe embracing them. The air is filled with pungent odors from the bubbling soup, and clouds of steam rise from the other cook-pots. On a long table are pyramids of bread, cut into cubes three or four inches square, usually rye or black bread, such as the natives of Norway prefer. Along the walls are deep cupboards containing the linens, the culinary supplies and utensils. In an adjoining but detached building is a furnace and boiler-room which furnishes the steam, and beside it a laundry and dish-washing establishment. It requires a good many dishes to serve three thousand people even in a simple way. In an annex the finer qualities of beef, mutton, and other meats are cut off and sold to the public, thus utilizing all the supplies which are bought in large quantities, the beef by the carcass and the vegetables by the carload. The sausage of the "Steam Kitchen" is said to be the best to be found in Christiania. All kinds of prepared meats are also sold in this annex butcher shop. During the fruit season the company runs a canning department upstairs, preserving all kinds of fruits, jellies, pickles, and that sort of thing. At the baking department bread is sold to the general public at wholesale or retail, and small retail establishments are supplied with all kinds of groceries as well as meats and other edibles. Thus the restaurant is only part of this large business from which the company derives its profits. There is naturally a good deal of jealousy among the competing small dealers against the "Steam Kitchen," but it serves a benevolent purpose, and there is no disposition among its customers to question its business methods or reduce its profits. It has succeeded in abolishing the cheap restaurants such as are found in all large cities, at which wretched food, generally the scrapings from high-class hotels and eating-houses, is worked over and sold to the poor.

It is an interesting sight, this bucket brigade, that stands in line and passes slowly by the serving windows, which are attended by half a dozen brawny Norwegian women with bare arms and broad, good-natured-looking faces. They wear neat white aprons and caps, and handle the food with a dexterity that shows long experience. They seem to know most of the customers and carry on a familiar conversation with them while falling their orders. When a bucket and a ticket passes up, blue for a nine-cent and red for a seven-cent dinner, the waitress first plunges a huge ladle into the soup pot and empties its contents into the bucket; then passing along the rows of kettles she harpoons a piece of meat with a long two-pronged fork, scoops up a quart of rice with a wooden shovel, and then, adding a portion of potatoes, slams on the cover, and, grabbing a cube of bread, passes it over to the purchaser with a joke or a few pleasant words.

Many of the customers are well dressed, according to the Norway standard, but no people in the world seem to care so little for their personal appearance, except on Sundays, when you can scarcely recognize men and women you have been familiar with during the week. On the day I ate at the restaurant, my cicerone pointed out at the dining table two professors of the University faculty, a lawyer in good standing, a photographer, and a sub-editor of one of the daily papers, who were his personal acquaintances. The remainder of the customers appeared to be professional men, clerks, bookkeepers, and a good many laborers, many of them coming for their dinner without having removed the traces of toil from their faces and hands. At one of the tables was a group of students inclined to be boisterous and evidently enjoying themselves. The "Steam Kitchen" is the favorite eating-place for the undergraduates, from four to five hundred being served every day.

Such an institution as the "Steam Kitchen" is especially suitable to a Norwegian city, where a portion of the population work for very small wages, the average income of the wage-earner being less than $100 a year—so small that, measured by the American standard, it would seem a difficult problem to find food, clothing, and shelter for a family.

Few Norwegians suffer from poverty or privation, even through the cold and gloomy winters that are eight months long. Our own people might die, or at least suffer seriously under the same circumstances, but the Norwegians are a hardy race. They have inherited the power of endurance and the ability to survive hunger and thirst and discomforts better than most races.

There are comparatively few poor in Sweden, probably fewer than in any other European country except Norway and Switzerland, because of the low cost of living, the sparse population, and the ability of all men and women to find work if they are willing to earn their own subsistence. Able-bodied paupers are compelled to work upon poor farms, but the aged, decrepit and invalids who are dependent upon public charity are kindly taken care of by what is called outdoor and indoor relief. In the cities are asylums and almshouses similar to those in the United States, but in the parishes, as a rule, the care of the poor is assigned to individual farmers and others who are willing to take care of them under contract, subject to the supervision of a board of guardians, of which the pastor is the chairman and the elders of the church are members. This has long been a practice in Sweden, but is not universal.

There are at present 5,277 relief establishments of all kinds in the kingdom, and the total contributions for the benefit of the poor amount to $3,000,000 annually, or on an average of 58 cents per capita of the entire population, an average of 44 cents in the country and $1.18 in the cities. This includes all poorhouses, asylums, hospitals, and other institutions for adults and children who can not take care of themselves.

A large part of the relief work in the cities is looked after by the Salvation Army under contract with the municipal authorities, but there are many institutions, hospitals, asylums, homes for the friendless and aged and for orphan children, supported by private charity. The free hospital for children in Stockholm is famous as one of the best equipped and managed institutions in the world.

The private charities in Stockholm are united for cooperation in an organization similar to those found in American cities, and all charitable institutions are subject to government supervision.[1]

CHAPTER XIII
MATERIAL CONDITIONS

The chief occupation of the Scandinavian peninsula is agriculture, employing more men and yielding larger monetary returns than any other industry in either Norway or Sweden. This may seem strange when it is recalled that sixty per cent of the surface of Norway is occupied by bare mountains, twenty-one per cent by woodlands, eight per cent by grazing lands, four per cent by lakes, and two per cent by ice fields, leaving only seven-tenths of one per cent for meadows and cultivated fields. And yet, the products of the farm equal the combined returns from shipping, lumber, and fisheries.

In Sweden the proportion of land under cultivation is considerably larger, the arable lands consisting of about twelve per cent of the total area, and in Sweden as in Norway, the agricultural products are more than those from shipping, lumber, and fisheries combined.

Nine-tenths of the farms of Norway and Sweden are owned by small proprietors; and although the right to dispose of landed property is relatively free, the laws of the country favor the retention of the farms in the families possessing them. An old allodial right makes it possible to redeem at an appraised value a farm that has been sold. This right is acquired after the property has belonged to the family for twenty years, but it is lost after the farm has been in the possession of strangers for three years. There are some farms that have been worked for a thousand years by the descendants of the same family. The best farms are about the banks of the lakes and in the narrow river valleys, and there are many fertile meadows which have never been plowed or put under cultivation, so that there are great future possibilities for tillage. And yet these meadows furnish fine hay-crops, and every blade of grass represents money in Scandinavia.

In a country extending through thirteen degrees of latitude, one might naturally expect a wide range of agricultural products. In the southeastern part of the peninsula most of the plants and orchard fruits of central Europe are found; whereas in the northern sections it is impossible to grow even the most hardy plants. Oats, barley, and rye are the chief cereals, but their production scarcely meets the needs of the country. Potatoes are the only root crops extensively cultivated. While the summers are short, vegetables and small fruit do excellently during the long, sun-lit hours. Scandinavians, however, do not seem habituated to a vegetable diet, and the cultivation of root plants seems very generally neglected. Pears, cherries, apples, raspberries, gooseberries, and currants may be grown under favorable conditions; but they play a minor role in Scandinavian horticulture.

The cow is a staple of wealth to the people of Scandinavia. They are diminutive in size, dun-colored, docile in habits, and excellent milk producers. It is said when they are well-fed they average from six to nine hundred gallons of milk a year. The mountain saeters, or dairies as we would call them, are the centers of the butter and cheese industry during the summer months.

The peninsula is also supplied with an excellent breed of small but hardy horses. The cream-colored fjord horses of Norway are only sixty inches high. They are active, hardy, and gentle; and in the mountainous parts of the country they are vastly more serviceable than mules would be. The Gudbrandsdalen breed, found chiefly in the mountain valleys, are larger than the fjord horses, and they are generally brown or black in color. Good horses bring surprisingly high prices. Working horses cost from $200 to $350 and the best stallions bring as much as $2,500.

The agricultural interests of Norway have suffered unmistakably by the enormous emigration to the United States. Two-thirds of the Norwegians of the world live in Iowa, Wisconsin, Minnesota, and the Dakotas. Nearly every Norwegian farmstead has kinsmen in our country; and the strong and vigorous always emigrate, thus leaving the farms at home in the hands of the old and infirm. America has been greatly benefited by this almost incessant exodus; for the Norse peasants have, without an exception, made splendid citizens, the best, in fact, that have come to us from Europe.

Commenting on the enormous emigration from the Norwegian farms, William Eleroy Curtis remarks:

"Notwithstanding the large emigration of young people, for whom the Norwegian farms are too small, it is apparent that the development of Norway is continually progressing along the highest lines, and that the tendency of the people, is upward socially and industrially, in culture and in wealth. The population of the kingdom not only holds its own, but shows a slight increase which seems remarkable because of the continual drain of young, able-bodied men and women who have removed to our western states. In all public movements, in all social, commercial, and industrial activities, in art, science, and literature, in wealth and prosperity, Norway stands abreast of the most advanced nations of Europe; but its progress is not won without greater effort than any other people put forth, and the application of thrift and industry elsewhere unknown, but which is required in a climate so bleak and inhospitable, and by a soil so wild and rocky. None but a race like the Norsemen could have kept a foothold here."

Norwegian economists recognize the loss to the country through emigration, and in recent years the national parliament has attempted to improve the condition of agricultural laborers. A fund of $135,000 has been set aside by the government for the purchase of land. Loans are granted to municipalities (1) for the purpose of buying large estates to be assigned to people without means at the purchase price, in plots of not more than twelve acres of tillable soil, and (2) for the purpose of being granted as loans on the security of parcels of the same size, which people without means may acquire as freehold property. The interest on these loans is from three to four per cent, and the time of payment is up to twenty-five years.

There is also a cultivation fund of $270,000, from which loans are granted for the purpose of cultivating and draining the soil. The interest is two and one-half per cent, and the time of repayment is up to twenty years, including five years in which no instalments are required. Such loans are granted (1) on the security of mortgages and (2) on the guaranty of the municipality.

Agricultural societies—national and county—receive government grants for the purpose of holding meetings and issuing documents that might be of service to farmers. There is also a staff of surveyors paid by the state to assist in the public allotment of land and otherwise to render assistance to needy lot-owners.

Considerable attention is also being given to the matter of agricultural education. Connected with the state agricultural college is an experimental farm, where not only farmers but also dairymen, gardeners, and foresters receive practical instruction.

Connected with the larger farms of Norway and Sweden are cotters' places—farm laborers who have leased a small part of the farm for a definite period (often during their natural lives). In some cases the cotter leases only a building with a garden attached; in other cases several acres of ground. The cotter is usually required to work on the farm of the owner at certain times of the year for a small wage regulated by contract. These cotters correspond to our truck farmers, and their plots of ground number about 35,000 on the outskirts of the cities and villages. They raise potatoes and other vegetables, and hay enough to feed a horse and several cows. In most cases the women and children do the work, while the men are engaged in other occupations. It is no longer permitted to establish entails which can not be sold or mortgaged, and the national government in recent years has sought to further the partition and allotment of the common ownership of land. Pastures and grazing lands are still often held by the community, and similarly mountain pastures. But the community farms, when the consent of all the part owners and tenants has been secured, may now be partitioned by surveyors appointed by the public authorities.

In the great timber districts of the mountain ranges, the trees are felled in winter and the logs are dragged to the tops of the steep mountain sides, where they are slid down to the river, or they are carted on sledges to the river's edge. During the early summer, after the ice has gone, and while the rivers are yet full of water, they are floated down the streams to the sawmills. But, as the logs are constantly being driven into corners or lodging against piers, floaters are employed to keep the logs in the current. Log-floating is both the most dangerous and the most unhealthful occupation in Norway. Men often fall into the streams; they are forced to sleep on the cold ground in uninhabited parts of the country; they frequently fall from the rolling logs into the whirling currents and are tossed against sharp rocks; and the marvel is not that the death-rate among floaters is so high, but that any of them survive the perilous occupation.

The value of the exports of forest products and timber industries reaches about eighteen million dollars a year, and the combined forest industries furnish employment to a large number of laborers. The state forests occupy about 3,500 square miles, more than half being located in the northern provinces of Tromsö and Finmark. The state also has nurseries at Vossevangen and Hamar, and three forestry schools, by means of which widespread interest in tree-planting has been aroused. Destructive forest fires and the slaughter of the trees by the remarkable development of the wood-pulp industries have emphasized in recent times the need of larger forest reserves and closer government supervision. Under the most favorable conditions, the pine requires from seventy-five to one hundred years to yield timber twenty-five feet in length and ten inches in diameter at the top. Spruce will reach the same size in seventy-five to eighty years. In the higher altitudes of the central part of the country the pine requires one hundred and fifty years, and rarely exceeds one hundred feet in height, and it decreases toward the coast and northwards.

The fisheries of Norway are among the most important in the world, yielding the nation more than seven million dollars a year, and furnishing employment to eighty thousand men. The sea-fisheries play the chief part in this branch of industry. The long coast line and the great ocean depth near the coast combine to give the fisheries of Norway unusual advantages. The abundance of fish is also due to the presence of masses of glutinous matter, apparently living protoplasm, which furnishes nutriment for millions of animalcules which again become food for the herring and other fish. The fish are mainly of the round sort found in deep waters, the cod, herring, and mackerel being the most important.

The cod yields the largest monetary returns. This fish migrates to the coast of Norway to spawn and in search of food. The best cod fisheries are in Romsdal, Nordland, and Tromsö counties, the Lofoten islands in Tromsö alone furnishing employment to more than four thousand men. The cod weighs from eight to twenty pounds and measures from five to six feet in length. Some are merely dried after having been cleaned. This is done by hanging them by the tail on wooden frames. The others are sent to the salting stations where they are salted and dried on flat rocks. A fish weighing ten pounds will yield two pounds of salted cod, the loss being due to the removal of the head and entrails and the drying out of the water.

There are numerous secondary products from the cod, the most valuable being the cod liver oil. The livers of the fish are exposed to a jet of superheated steam which destroys the liver cells and causes the small drops of oil to run together. The roe are salted and sent to France to be used for bait in the sardine fisheries.

In the matter of the handicraft industries carried on in the homes, Norway has long taken high rank. As early as the ninth century her artisans were skilled in the manufacture of arms, farming implements, and boats, and her women in cloth weaving and embroidery. During recent times the ease and cheapness with which foreign products could be obtained caused a marked decline in home industries; but at the present moment an effort is being made to rehabilitate them through a national domestic industry association, organized in 1891, which has taken up the manufacture of hand-carved articles, sheath-knives, skis, sledges, and woven and embroidered woolen and linen goods after the old Norwegian patterns.

The manufacture of lumber and wooden ware is one of the leading industrial pursuits. With the exception of the two most northern counties, practically every section of the country is represented by sawmills and planing mills. Ship-building in recent times has attained considerable importance, and the manufacture of paper of the chemical wood-pulp variety has become one of the leading industries. There are a few cloth, rope, and jersey mills at Bergen and Christiania, but the textile industries of Norway are relatively unimportant. On the other hand, leather, India rubber, glass, metal, and chemical industries have become important of late years.

Norway is not rich in mineral products. The combined mining industries do not yield more than two million dollars a year, and they furnish employment to less than four thousand men. The Kongsberg silver mines have been operated for more than three hundred years, but the recent fall in the price of silver has reduced the output. The copper mines at Rorös have been operated for two hundred and fifty years, and there are less important copper mines in Nordland, Telemarken, and the Hardanger. There are iron mines at Arendal and elsewhere, but the rise in the cost of charcoal, due to the scarcity of wood, has greatly crippled the iron industry. There are important soapstone quarries in the Gudbransdal and the Trondhjem basin; green colored slate in the Valders and at Vossevangen; and granite, syenite, and porphyry in many parts of the country.

Measured by population and national wealth, the commerce of Norway is relatively important, due in a large measure to her enormous merchant marine and the efficiency of her hardy seamen. Relatively to the population of the country, Norway has the largest merchant fleet in the world, and in the matter of steamships and sailing vessels she is surpassed only by three countries—Great Britain, Germany, and the United States. Not only is her fleet large, but her service is efficient. Norwegian seamen the world over are esteemed for ability and honesty, inspiring all commercial nations with confidence that goods carried in Norse bottoms will be carefully and conscientiously treated; and her seamen are everywhere sought to man foreign vessels.

In industries, the Swedes excel in the manufacture of iron. To fully appreciate the value of this industry, one should visit Gefle, the most important shipping point on the eastern coast of Sweden. Here there is a fine harbor, with docks and warehouses owned by the government. From this port the ore from the mines of central Sweden is shipped to all parts of the world and handled by Brown hoisting machinery, which is made in Cleveland, Ohio—the same that you see on the ore docks at South Chicago and at Cleveland, Buffalo, Ashtabula, and other points on the Great Lakes where iron ore and coal are handled.

At Gefle, too, an annual industrial exposition is held, where you may see on exhibit all the utensils manufactured or used by the people—all kinds of machinery, tools, and implements, recent novelties in patents, weaving, wood-carving, and a large part of the exposition building is given up to beautiful articles in iron, in the manufacture of which we have said the Swedes excel.

A little west of Gefle is the town of Fahlun, which is the headquarters of the Kopparberg Mining Company, the, oldest industrial corporation in the world. The buildings date back to the seventeenth century and the mines are even more ancient. A mortgage bond was filed upon them in the year 1288 by a German company, and the records show that in 1347 the privilege of working them was sold by the king of Sweden to a syndicate of Lubeck miners. But these documents which are on file in the archives of the town are comparatively modern, because the copper deposits at Fahlun were known and worked in prehistoric times, and from them the Vikings obtained the sheathings for their ships and the material from which their copper armor, implements, and utensils were made. An immense amount of copper was used and worked with great skill in Scandinavia even before the Christian era, and the most of it came from the great deposits at Fahlun.

The iron industry is old in Sweden. Isaac Breant, a tradesman in Stockholm, founded a company and received a charter from Charles XI in 1685. He built the first blast furnace in Sweden, and died in 1702, leaving the property to his son, who died in 1720. The heirs sold out in 1722 to a man named Grill, in whose family the property remained until 1800, when it was purchased by the ancestors of the present owners.

The famous Dannemora mines, which produce the best Bessemer ore in the world, have been worked continuously since 1481. It is one of the most valuable and extensive iron deposits in the world, and resembles those of Lake Superior. The area of ore already located covers 12,500 square meters. [m]

CHAPTER XIV
HIGHWAYS, RAILWAYS, AND WATERWAYS

Since the sixteenth century Norway has had an excellent public posting system which enables the traveler to go to the most remote parts of the country at moderate and fixed rates. Fast and slow posting stations are established by the government along all the national highways. At the former, horses must be kept in readiness; whereas, at the latter, the horses may be in distant fields at work, and a couple of hours may elapse before the traveler can proceed upon his journey. The rates, which are determined by the government, are, from fast stations, about seven cents a mile for a horse and two-wheeled conveyance or sledge; but from slow stations they are scarcely more than half that price. When the road is over very steep mountains, an extra fare is charged, usually double; but this is a government regulation and is always understood. The posting stations are, for the most part, isolated and solitary farms. The farmers undertake to provide rooms and meals, as well as drivers, horses, and conveyances. Stations are usually from seven to fifteen miles apart, and farmers are required to convey the traveler only as far as the next station.

Two kinds of wagons are used, the carriole and the stolkjaerre. The carriole resembles an American sulky, except that it is springless, and nearly the entire weight is forward of the axle. It is a two-wheeled gig with the body shaped like the bowl of a spoon. The seat, in front of the axletree, is fastened by cross-pieces to the long, slender shafts that project behind and provide a place for light luggage and a seat for the driver. The carriole is for one passenger. It is falling into disuse, and its place is being taken by the stolkjaerre, a two-wheeled cart that will carry two passengers. It also has long shafts which extend under the axletree to make a support for the luggage and a seat for the driver. The passenger's seat is in front, perched on two wooden bars stretched obliquely upwards and backwards from the front of the vehicle. The drivers, usually men although sometimes girls, vary in age from six to sixty years.

The Norwegian horses are stout, stubby, and spirited little beasts. They are cream-colored, high crested, and have black manes and tails; the manes are cropped, except the forelocks, which are left to protect the eyes from the sun, and the tails are very full. Horses are valued in Norway by the size and fullness of their tails. These little animals are so trustworthy and intelligent that tourists, as well as peasants, soon get to look upon them as companions. In every "skyds-station," as the posting stations are called, in a conspicuous place is posted this inscription: *Vaer god mod hesten*. This means "be good to the horse." At every station there is also a book, called the *skydsbog*, in which travelers are requested to write their names and any complaints they may have to make regarding their treatment. At intervals these books are examined by government officials.

Swedish horses are much larger than those of Norway, tall, heavy, with long legs and barrel-shaped bodies, very much like Canadian stock. They drive well, make good speed, and will eat anything. At the livery stables one can hire outfits by the day or hour—the legal price being 63 cents an hour or 56 cents to any point within the city limits, and there is an excellent cab system, with what is known as the "taxameter" register. Every cab is equipped with an arrangement similar to a gas meter, which shows on a dial the money due, whether you are using it by the hour or by the distance. The hackman sets his clock at zero at the time of starting, according to the number of passengers or whether he is hired by time or distance, and it ticks away while you ride or while he waits. The fare for one or two persons is sixty-two cents per hour; for three persons, eighty-seven cents an hour; for four persons, $1.24 and a tip to the driver anywhere from one cent to fifteen cents, according to the time he has been with you. The public posting system outside of the cities is similar to that of Norway.

The national government builds the main highways, while the cross roads are built by the parishes. The management is in the hands of a bureau in the national department of public works, and the maintenance falls upon the people who live in the neighborhood, under the supervision of a local inspector. Every farmer has a piece of road to take care of, according to the amount of land he owns, and at intervals slabs of cast iron are erected bearing his name and the section of the road he is to keep in order. Thus every man's reputation is at stake in the neighborhood, and if there is a muddy place or a rut, everybody knows who is to blame for it, and it can not be laid to the county commissioner, as is the case in America. On the outside of each road is a line of large blocks of stone set upright, which serves as a barrier to prevent wagons from going off into the ditch. There are 6,500 miles of main highway, and 11,000 miles of cross-road, or a total of 17,500 miles of roads in Norway, and the total expenditure upon them by national and local authorities will average a million and a half dollars every year.

The first cost of a road is usually about $3,000 a mile. They first dig an excavation about three feet deep, as if they were going to make a canal. On the bottom are thrown heavy blocks of stone through which the water can filter, and occasionally there is a little drain to carry it off. Upon this is a layer of smaller stones, and then still smaller, until the surfacing is reached, which is macadam of pounded slate, mixed with gravel and stone.

During the winter the farmers have to keep their several sections free from snow, but to do this it is necessary for them to co-operate, for it would be impossible for one family to handle the heavy plows that are necessary. Six, eight, and ten horses are often hitched to them—all the horses in the neighborhood—and it is often the work of weeks instead of days to get the roads opened up for travel, but when it is once done, it is as clear and smooth for sleighs as a city boulevard.

Norway has only one mile of railway for every one hundred square miles of land; but the mountainous character of the country, the heavy snowfall during the long winters, and the thin, scattered population make railway construction almost prohibitive. Nevertheless, the new kingdom has made a commendable beginning, and the state has plans for enormous extensions during the next twenty-five years. There are now nine railway lines in the country, with a total mileage of one thousand five hundred and eighty-four, but half of which is broad gauge. The state railways have been constructed partly by subscriptions taken in the districts interested in the construction of new lines, and partly at the expense of the national government.

The leading railway lines radiate from Christiania to Stockholm, Goteborg, Trondhjem, Gudbransdal, Telemarken, and the Valders. The longest line—three hundred and fifty miles—is from Christiania to Trondhjem through Hamar. There is also a relatively long line—one hundred and ninety miles—from Christiania up the Gudbrandsdal by Lake Mjosen and through Lillehammer to Otta. In 1906, the Valders railway, connecting Christiania with Fagernaes—a distance of one hundred and thirty-one miles—was opened. This connects with the most important of the new roads being built, the one from Christiania to Bergen. This road will reach entirely across the country, from Christiania on the Swedish frontier to Bergen on the Atlantic coast, thus making connection between the two largest cities of Norway, journeys between which are now only possible by steamships and carriages, consuming from three to six days.

The new road goes through the mountains and presents many engineering difficulties. Two-thirds of the way the roadbed must be cut out of the mountain side, and there is a tunnel three miles long at a height of two thousand eight hundred and twenty feet above the sea level. The snow in the winter is so heavy that it will be necessary to cover the tracks with sheds for a distance of nearly sixty miles. The construction is not only difficult, but expensive, and although the distance is but three hundred and ten miles, it will be one of the most costly railroads ever built. Sixty-seven miles of the line between Bergen and Vose, on the western coast, is already in operation, and it is a favorite journey of tourists, for the scenery is superb, although the traveler is in a tunnel one-tenth of the entire distance. There are forty-eight tunnels in all. A shelf has been hewn and blasted along the side of the mountains that encloses the celebrated Sorfjord.

The Norwegians call a railway a *jernbane*, literally "an iron path." Their cars are made on the conventional European pattern, and are light and comfortable. They are furnished with toilet rooms, and run smoothly and noiselessly. Most of the trains are equipped with Westinghouse brakes, steam heat, and electric lights. The trains run very slowly. Economy is studied in this respect, as in every other. There is a certain speed—say, fifteen or eighteen miles an hour—which can be maintained at a minimum consumption of fuel, and the Scandinavian railway managers have figured it down to a dot. They can haul a longer train a greater distance with a ton of coal than any other engineers, and the most scrupulous attention is applied to every feature of management, the tracks, the rolling stock, the station, the crossings. The crossing-keepers are usually women. A large number of that sex are employed by the railways.

The stops at the stations seem unnecessarily long to impatient Americans, but the time is utilized by the leisurely passengers in drinking big goblets of beer, and by the conductor in parading up and down the platform so that the patrons of the road can have an opportunity to admire his radiant uniform and fine shape. In Scandinavian countries the best-looking men seem to have been selected for railway conductors and policemen, and their deportment is decidedly different from what we are used to in America. If you ask a question of a Norwegian policeman, he will bring his heels together, give a military salute, and stand in the attitude of attention like a soldier while he answers. He usually understands English, too, and those who can not are remarkably accurate guessers, and all take a friendly interest in your inquiries instead of giving you a short answer and a cold shoulder like the policemen in our cities. They will walk to the corner to point out the house in the middle of the next block if that is where you want to go, and when you thank them for their attention, you get another salute that makes you feel as big as a major general, or as if you had been mistaken for a member of the royal family. Railway conductors are equally polite, and seem to understand that it is a part of their business to protect tender-footed travelers, as angels always look after good little boys.

In southern Sweden there is scarcely a parish without a railway, and in the northern part of the kingdom, where the railway facilities are limited, posting stations are maintained by the government similar to those in Norway. There is a railway running as far north as the 67th parallel of latitude, about fifty miles beyond the polar circle into Lapland, to the famous mines of Malmberget, with a branch to Trondhjem, Norway. The line follows the coast of the Gulf of Bothnia very closely, through a country well covered with small pine timber, which was being rapidly stripped until the government interfered by passing rigid regulations and appointing foresters to enforce them.

You can see the midnight sun from several places on this railway, anywhere above 66 degrees and 33 minutes of latitude, from the 9th of June to the 3d of July, and farther north for a longer period. At Gellivare the midnight sun can be seen regularly from June 5 to July 11, and it is a much more convenient and quicker journey than to the North Cape and other polar resorts in Norway. During that period a traveler is reasonably certain of seeing the sun at all hours of the day as long as he cares to stay, while over in Norway that privilege is rare and uncertain, owing to the fogs and clouds that obscure the horizon sometimes for days at a time. But there is nothing else to call the tourist to this part of Sweden, for the scenery is monotonous and uninteresting and the facilities for travel are primitive and the tourists are few.

Everybody who has taken the trouble to make the journey, of course, advises other people to do the same, and insists that it is worth the time, money, and fatigue it costs, on the same principle as the fox that lost his tail in a trap wanted all the other foxes to cut off their tails. There is one train each way daily, but it runs very slowly,—about fifteen or eighteen miles an hour,—and stops a long time at the stations. The cars are comfortable. The road belongs to the government, and was built in the '90's for the transportation of ore from the iron mines, which was previously hauled by cart in summer and reindeer sledges in winter, to the ports of Lulea and Allapen, a distance of about one hundred and forty miles.

When it is recalled that two-thirds of the inhabitants of Norway live upon the coasts and fjords, the large part which water traffic plays in the economy of the country will be easily understood. The coast being well protected by a chain of islands, the skjaergaard, both travel and commerce are carried on by means of small open boats. The fjord rowboats, as a rule, are light and pointed, with upright and high prow, and they carry a square sail. They are light to row, and they go capitally before the wind. There is an extensive government posting system on the coasts, fjords, and inland lakes, similar to that along the public highways already described. The tariff from fast stations for a four-oared boat and sail with two rowers is about twelve cents a mile; eighteen cents for three rowers and a six-oared boat, and twenty-four cents a mile for a boat with eight oars and four rowers. The tariff is decided by the size of the boat and not by the number of passengers. The rowers are not infrequently girls and women.

The large fjords and lakes have ample steamboat facilities, the coast service between Bergen and Trondhjem being especially good. The navigable channels of the fjords represent a coast line of twelve thousand miles, and they are so entirely separated from the sea by islands and reefs and obstructed at their entrances by old moraines, that the fresh water from the melting snows and rivers lies four or five feet deep on the surface. Small steamers ply on all the larger fjords on which the rates are moderate and the accommodations fair. On most of these boats a passenger pays full fare for himself and half fare for the other members of his family, including his wife. Persons who want to see the fjords of Norway thoroughly should take the regular mail steamers, which call at all small ports and take a month instead of a week for the voyage. The boats are small, but clean and comfortable, and only occasionally have bad weather—very seldom in summer. They wind in and out of the narrow passages, and because of their size can navigate where the larger tourist steamers are not able to go, and therefore the passengers on the latter miss some of the finest scenery.

Voyages to the North Cape by the tourist steamers are limited to a few weeks during the midsummer, when the sun is supposed to be visible at midnight in the arctic regions, but steamers run regularly all the year way around the Cape to Archangel, Vadsö, and Horningsvaag, the arctic ports of Russia. The fjords never freeze, so that navigation is always open, and there is more or less travel in midwinter between the civilized portions of the arctic regions.

If you will take your map and examine the north coast of Europe within the arctic circle, you will find several towns east of the North Cape on the White Sea which are wide open 365 days in the year, and do more business in the winter than during the summer months. They do not see the sun from December to February. At some places it is invisible for a longer period, but at Hammerfest the streets, houses, and business places are lighted with electric lights, and similar plants are being introduced into other cities of the polar section. It is stated, also, that the aurora borealis is so brilliant night after night as to make it easy to read ordinary newspaper print without artificial light, and by long experience people are prepared for the peculiar conditions that exist there. The passengers on the steamers in these waters in winter are mostly commercial travelers and men interested in the fisheries, which are more active from October to March than at any other time of the year.

There are also two canals in Norway that are used for passenger traffic—the Fredrikshald canal, connecting the Femsjöen and Skullerud lakes, and the Skien-Nordsjö-Bandak canal, connecting the Nordsjö lake with the Hitterdal and Bandak lakes. Between the Hitterdal and the Nordsjö lake there is a rise of fifty feet, which is overcome by two locks at Skien and four at Loveid; and between the Nordsjö and the Bandak lakes there is a rise of one hundred and eighty-seven feet, which is overcome by fourteen locks, five of which are around a waterfall, the Vrangfos, where the average rise for each lock is about thirteen feet. The postal, telegraph, and telephone systems, all under government control, are both cheaper and more efficient than in the United States, where the two latter are private monopolies. With the exception of Switzerland, Norway is more abundantly supplied with postoffices, in proportion to her size, than any other country in the international postal union. The length of her telegraph lines, in relation to the population of the country is greater than in any other country. There is no place in the world where telephones are so cheap or so numerous as in Stockholm. There are more telephones in Stockholm than in Berlin or London, and it is contended that there are more than in Paris, but that is doubtful. The total number of instruments in use is nearly 50,000 to a population of 300,000. You can find a telephone in every shop and in almost every house, and in the parks and on the street corners on lamp posts are little booths similar to those used for police boxes in the cities of the United States. They work automatically. You drop a little coin worth three cents into the slot, and then ring the bell. For several years every room in the principal hotels has had its own telephone, on the same system that has recently been introduced into the United States, and upon some of the steamers sailing from Stockholm there is a telephone in every stateroom. The long distance 'phones and all the lines outside of two or three of the principal cities belong to the government and are operated by the Postoffice Department. The rents vary from $10 to $28 a year.

The telegraph system is owned by the government, which charges a uniform rate of fifteen cents for ten words to any part of the country.

CHAPTER XV
THE PEOPLE: THEIR MANNERS AND CUSTOMS

Because of its geographic isolation, the Scandinavian peninsula is the home of the purest Teutonic ethnic stock. The Norwegians, Icelanders, Swedes, and Danes are racially closely related, and they belong to the same branch of the Aryan family as the Germans, Flemish, English, and Anglo-Americans. Physically, these people are powerfully built and tall, of the pure Scandinavian type, with fair hair and blue eyes, and their healthy, intelligent look strikes the traveler. In addition to the physical characteristics held in common by these Scandinavian peoples, the Norwegians are to be specially noted for their long narrow heads, particularly is this so among the people in the interior of the country. Here, too, the stature is the greatest. During the Civil War in the United States, it was found that among the enlisted troops the Norwegians, after the Americans, had the greatest stature, and that in breadth of chest they were excelled by none. It is probably true, however, that the Norwegians who emigrate represent the finest physical types, and that they possess a higher average stature than one finds in Norway to-day, if the most northerly provinces are excepted.

The Norwegians are a very plain people—neither pretty nor handsome. The women are strong and square-built, and what beauty they have is of the solid and substantial sort. Of the two sexes, the men are the better proportioned, both in the matter of figures and features. They have light complexions,—barring the bronzing of the skin due to constant exposure,—light hair, blue eyes, and reasonably well-formed noses. Both men and women have frank and open countenances.

The most marked mental characteristics are clear insight, unconquerable pertinacity, dogged obstinacy, absolute honesty, and a sturdy sense of independence. Björnson has well remarked concerning his people: "Opinions are slowly formed and tenaciously held, and much independence is developed by the rigorous isolation of farm from farm each on its own freehold ground, unannoyed and uncontradicted by any one. The way the people work together in the fields, in the forests, and in their large rooms has given them a characteristic stamp of confidence in each other." It is perhaps this isolation that has perpetuated so many of the old customs and superstitions for which the Norwegians are noted.

William Eleroy Curtis tells of seeing the funeral of one of these Norway farmers:

"His house was trimmed with green boughs and festooned with ropes of flowers and ground pine. The word *farvel*, "farewell," was worked in green over the front door. The coffin, which was carried on a bier by the neighbors to the little cemetery not far away, was covered with flowers, and following it were a number of women clad in somber black with little white shawls tied under their chins, each carrying a wreath in her hands. The minister led the procession. He was dressed in a long black gown reaching to his heels, like the cassock of a Catholic priest; his hat was of felt, with a low crown and a broad brim, similar to those worn by the curates of the Church of England, while around his neck was a linen ruff that looked as if it might have been worn in the time of Queen Elizabeth.

"A grave had been dug in the churchyard. The neighbors who had borne the body, lowered it tenderly to the bottom, and when they had lifted the cover of the coffin in place, each man, the oldest first, threw in a shovelful of earth. All the women did not use the shovel, some of them took up handsful of soil and let it gently filter through their fingers into the open vault; and finally three children, somewhere about ten or eleven years of age, followed the example of their elders and added their little share to the brown coverlid of the dead. The pastor removed his hat, extended his arms and pronounced a benediction. Then the women laid their wreaths on the newly covered grave and sorrowfully turned homeward."

Independence and frankness characterize all classes of society. Norway has no hereditary aristocracy. In 1821 it was provided that those holding titles might be allowed to retain them during their lives, but they could not transmit them to their children. The Norse character has never been marred by the yoke of slavery. The feudal system, with its serfdom, never got a footing in the north. The people have always been small landholders, which has developed among them an independence of character not found in countries where the mass of the inhabitants have no direct property interests. There is no class in Norway corresponding to the country gentleman of England or to the grand seigneurs and provincial noblemen of the Continent. The wealthiest landlord is only a peasant.

Honesty is one of the valuable assets of the Norwegian people. Attempts at extortion are so rare that tourists, accustomed to the proverbial dishonesty of the Latin races, find travel in Norway and Sweden a joy. An English traveler relates this typical incident: He had lost his purse shortly after leaving Vossevangen for Stalheim. Altogether unconscious of his loss, he walked on placidly. Suddenly hearing hurried footsteps following him, he turned about and faced a lad who thrust the pocketbook into the owner's hand and disappeared before the Englishman could get a coin from his pocket to reward the boy for his honesty. The Norwegian boy very properly did not expect a reward for doing the only thing open to his mind upon finding the purse.

> Kindness to animals is another virtue of the Norwegian people.
>
> Illustrating this trait we again quote William Eleroy Curtis:
>
> "There seems to be a close relation between the human kind and their animals. The men and women talk to the horses and cattle as if they were understood. We had a *skydsgut*, or driver, one day, who held continuous conversation with his horses. Every time he would come to a hill he would walk beside them and talk to them all the way up in a gentle, caressing sort of way, like a child talking to a doll, and once when he stopped for water and the near horse wanted to drink more than the driver thought was good for him, he scolded like an old woman. The horse shook his head and rattled his harness impatiently, as much as to say, 'You get back onto your box and attend to your business and I'll attend to mine.'"

That intellectuality is one of the traits of the Swedes and Norwegians alike is evidenced in the long list of names that have become famous in the world's literature. In spite of the high intellectual attainments of these people, they are fond of the quiet, simple life, with friends and kinsfolk and home employments and home enjoyments. And they are very superstitious, too, and, in spite of their Lutheran faith, they have never discarded the customs that grew from belief in gods many, and fairies, trolls, gnomes and norns without number. The forests, the mountains and gorges, are inhabited by these people still. Nissen is the good fairy of the farmers. He looks after the cattle particularly, and if he is well treated they are healthy, and the cows give lots of milk. To propitiate him it is necessary to put a dish of porridge on the threshold of the cow stable on Christmas morning. Whenever the family move, this invisible being goes along with them and sits on the top of the loads. In haying time he always rides on the load of hay, and the *bedstemoder*, best mother or grandmother, in every farmhouse can tell the children dozens of interesting stories about the mischief or the kindness of Nissen.

He is invariably represented in pictures of farm life; he appears on the illustrated advertisements of farm machinery; his figure carved in wood is sold at all the curiosity stores, and he appears as a prominent character in most of the fairy stories that deal with farm life. He is represented as a short, fat, bow-legged man, with big whiskers and long white hair, wearing a red hat like those worn by clowns in circuses. He usually appears in his shirt sleeves, with an open collar, a blue vest, and knickerbockers upon his legs, which are as slim as those of a brownie. His circumference is greater than his height, and his head is almost as large as his body.

Noek is the fairy of the waterfalls and is a sort of merman. You never see more than half his body. He is very, very old, his hair and beard are long and white, and his face is always pale and pensive. He carries a harp and plays to amuse the spirits in the waterfall. A statue of Ole Bull has recently been erected in his native city of Bergen. He stands upon a pedestal which rises from a fountain, and the water flows over the head and shoulders of a Noek at the base.

Norway offers a fine field for reformers to study the effects of regulation upon the vice of drunkenness. Within the limits of the kingdom are all grades of restriction, from prohibition to liberal license. There are no pretensions about the Norwegians; there is no affectation about their morals and no leniency in the administration of their laws. The police and the magistrates are merciless and inexorable, and crime is punished more severely perhaps than in any other country. At the same time the people distinguish an important difference between temperance and total abstinence. They give their children beer in unlimited quantities, but absolutely prohibit the sale of whisky, and send drunken men to prison with burglars and assassins. Norwegian reformers hold that beer is the great promoter of temperance, and encourage its use as a beverage, although every saloon in the kingdom is closed on Sundays, on all holidays, and Saturday afternoon, which is the regular pay day for the working classes. These are practical regulations, devised for the purpose of restraining those who are not capable of controlling their own appetites and encouraging thrift and economy. While the saloons are closed on pay day, the savings banks are open until midnight.

It is difficult to become accustomed to the long twilights in Norway. One can read and write at a window as late as ten o'clock without difficulty, and during the months of June, July, and August few artificial lights are used, either in the streets or in the shops or in the residences. A candle is usually kept handy for an emergency, but it is light enough to dress and undress at any hour of the night, and it seems childish to go to bed before dark. The hours for meals are awkward to those accustomed to American ways. Breakfast is usually served from seven till nine o'clock. Four o'clock is the fashionable dinner hour, without luncheon. After dinner men return to their business and keep open their shops and offices until a nine or ten o'clock supper during the long days.

No one will ever starve to death in Norway. American palates may not always crave the food, but they can not complain of its abundance. The table is usually loaded with all sorts of fish and cold meats, both fresh and preserved, that foreigners are usually afraid of. The Norwegians are fond of things with a pronounced flavor, the more pronounced the better, and cheese is one of the chief articles of diet. A Norwegian housewife would not consider a meal complete without five or six different kinds of cheese of all degrees of pungency in taste and odor upon the table. At breakfast you are served sardines, anchovies, smoked salmon, dried herring and five or six other kinds of fish and an equal variety of cheese before they think of offering you coffee and meat and potatoes. You get seven or eight kinds of bread also, but it is all cold. The national bread, which is made of flour, water and a little salt, with a sprinkling of caraway seed, rolled very thin and punctured with holes like a cracker, is baked only once or twice a year, and then in large quantities, as New England women bake mince pies and put them on the top shelf to season. It is called *grovboröd*, and tastes like a water cracker.

The servant-girl problem has been solved in Norway to the satisfaction of all concerned, although it is doubtful whether a similar solution would be accepted by domestic servants in the United States. In large cities like Bergen and Christiania, there is a central employment bureau under the direction of the municipal government, and twice a year—one week before New Year's day and one week before St. John's day, the 24th of June—there is a general change of servants by those who are dissatisfied with existing conditions, and engagements are made for the ensuing six months of the year. Families who want servants, fill out blanks setting forth what is required and the wages they are willing to pay. These are filed at the employment office and are noted in a conspicuous manner upon a blackboard. Women or men in search of employment go to this bureau during the weeks named, examine the blackboard, and apply to the clerk in charge for further information.

If they desire to apply for a particular position, they submit their recommendations to the clerk, and if he is satisfied, he gives them a card to the lady of the house. That card is good for the day only, and must be returned by the lady of the house before the close of office hours. If the girl is engaged, the blanks upon the card are filled out with a general statement as to her duties, the term of service, and the wages agreed upon, and the card is filed away for reference if necessary. If the lady of the house is not satisfied with the applicant, she sends her away and returns the card marked "not satisfactory," with the request that other applicants be sent her. If the applicant is satisfactory, the lady of the house pays her a bonus of one krone or two kroner called "hand money"—that is, she crosses her hand with silver as an evidence of good faith—and the girl agrees to report for duty within one week after New Year's or Midsummer's day, as the case may be. That is to allow her present employer to fill her place. In some of the smaller towns the dates for changing servants are April 14 and October 14.

The law protects both the employer and the employed. The employer guarantees to give the servant a comfortable room, wholesome food, take care of her if sick, and pay her wages regularly as agreed upon during good behavior; while the girl agrees to perform her duties faithfully during the term for which she is engaged. If there is any complaint upon either side, it must be made to a magistrate, who investigates and decides between them. A family can not get rid of a servant during her term of employment without official intervention. On the other hand, the girl's wages are a first lien upon their property for the entire term, although judgment must be rendered and made a matter of record. If a servant runs away from her employer, she can be arrested and fined. Cooks are paid from $4 to $7 a month; housemaids from $3 to $6 a month; men butlers from $10 to $15; coachmen from $12 to $16 a month; scullery maids and men of all work receive corresponding wages.

Nearly all of these domestic customs here related apply to Sweden as well as Norway, and there are many interesting additional ones. In Sweden the state dinners at the palace are always at six o'clock. At nearly all the other courts of Europe it is customary to dine at eight o'clock. The king's dinners are short, his guests seldom remaining more than an hour at the table, after which the ladies adjourn to one of the drawing rooms, the gentlemen to the smoking room, and later all are entertained by musicians from the opera house or the royal conservatory. Carriages are usually ordered at ten o'clock. This seems old-fashioned, but for people who like to go to bed early and those who are occupied with business all day it is much more sensible than the custom followed in some cities, where social festivities do not begin until the hour when the king of Sweden's guests are bidding him good night.

But everybody complains that the Swedes are drifting away from old customs and are becoming modernized. The French influence seems to prevail, and modern Swedish life is becoming an imitation of that of Paris.

Another of the old customs is for people to indicate their business upon their visiting cards. You will receive the card of Lawyer Jones, or Banker Smith, or Music Professor Smith, and so on; and these titles are also used in addressing them. It would seem rather queer for any one in the United States to ask, "Wholesale Merchant MacVeigh, will you kindly pass the butter?" or "Banker Hutchinson, will you escort Fru Board of Trade Operator Jones to the table?" But that is the custom in Sweden and it is observed by children as well as grown people. A lisping child will approach a guest, make a pretty little bob-courtesy, and say, "Good morning, Chief Justice of the Supreme Court Fuller," or "Good night, Representative in Congress Boutell." It is customary for ladies to print their maiden names upon their visiting cards in smaller type, under their married names, particularly if they have a pride of family and want people to know their ancestry.

To see the old Swedish customs that have almost entirely disappeared from the country, one must go to the hill districts of Dalecarlia, where the people are so unlike the rest of the Swedes in their dress, their customs and habits, and in many other respects as to almost seem another race.

The Dalecarlians are great dancers, and the social gatherings at their homes during the winter are always accompanied by that form of amusement. During the summer they dance in the open air. On St. John's Day the entire population, old and young, dance around a May-pole erected at some convenient place, and at harvest time, whenever the last sheaf in a field is pitched upon the cart or the stack, it is customary for somebody to produce a musical instrument, a violin, a nyckleharpa, a harmonicum, or perhaps only a mouth organ, and everybody—for the boys and girls of the family all work together in the hay and harvest fields—join in a dance before returning home.

The dances are original and often interesting. One of the most ancient and popular is the *däfva vadmal* (weaving homespun), whose figures are supposed to imitate the action of the shuttle, the beating in of the woof, and other motions used in weaving at an old-fashioned loom. Some of the dances resemble those of Scotland, and one is almost exactly like the Virginia reel as danced by old-fashioned people in the United States. In another, called the "garland," the dancers wind in and out under their clasped hands in imitation of the weaving of a wreath of flowers. All the dances require violent physical exercise, but the Swedish men and women are famous for muscular development. Some of the dances are accompanied by pretty melodies sung in unison by both sexes.

The songs of the Dalecarlian peasant are not lively, but rather slow in movement, and are usually sung in unison, the music being rarely arranged for parts.

Dalecarlia has a certain preeminence among the districts of Sweden because of the part its people have played in the history of the country, and however the other provinces may dispute among themselves about their claims for distinction, each will admit that Dalecarlia is entitled to special consideration. Its people represent the highest patriotism and the noblest characteristics of the Swedish race, and when any one is spoken of as a Dalecarlian, it means that he is a free and intelligent citizen of independent thought and action and lives a life of manly simplicity.[o]

CHAPTER XVI
HEALTH, EXERCISE, AND AMUSEMENTS

Perhaps in no other country in the world have health and exercise been united and formed into a national institution, as they have been in Sweden. The true Swede believes that exercise will cure everything, and that as a preventive of disease there is nothing like it. If you go to a Swedish physician for advice, he will invariably prescribe the movement cure, and send you to a gymnasium or a massage establishment instead of to a drug store. Physical exercise is therefore the national remedy, particularly for complaints due to sedentary employment, neglect of nature's laws, and high living. The movement cure for invalids, which is practically the same as that we have in the United States, is used in all the hospitals as well as in private practice. It was invented about a century ago by Dr. Ling, a patriot, a gymnast and a poet, who was inspired to revive the ancestral national spirit in the Swedish people by the aid of sports and songs, and to develop once more the great qualities of strength, courage, and endurance which in old times distinguished the Scandinavian race. After a hard struggle he succeeded, in 1814, in securing the recognition of the government and founded the Royal Gymnastic Central Institute, where all persons desiring to teach gymnastics in the public schools or in private institutions must take a course of training and take a degree. The Swedes are quite as particular about this as they are about the study of medicine. No medical practitioner can hang out a sign without a diploma from one of the universities, and no person can teach gymnastics in that country without a similar certificate of competency from the Royal Institute. Every officer of the army is required to undergo a course of instruction, not only to develop his physical constitution, but to qualify him to teach gymnastics to his soldiers. The teachers of physical culture in the public schools, both men and women, are obliged to take a similar course in order to drill their pupils properly, for in every schoolroom in the country, down to the kindergartens, daily physical exercise upon Ling's plan is required to promote the development of the body and improve the health. This is required in private as well as public schools, and the methods of instruction are subject to the inspection and approval of the Central Institute. In every town of any size there are gymnastic clubs and associations, which are generally guided by instructors educated at the Central Institute. They include women as well as men in their membership, and in many of them fencing and other sword exercises are also taught. In common with all the gymnasiums are bath-houses. You will find them in every part of the city of Stockholm and in other large towns. Some of them occupy entire buildings. It is the habit of business men to go to their stores or offices at nine o'clock in the morning and remain there until two or three in the afternoon, when they go to their club or gymnasium and take an hour's exercise and afterward a bath. These establishments in the business quarter of Stockholm and other cities are considered just as important as clubs, restaurants, or other places of resort, and usually have connected with them reading and smoking rooms where patrons can read the daily newspapers and current magazines and sip coffee and smoke while they are cooling off. It would surprise a visitor in New York or Chicago to be informed that his broker or his lawyer or his banker or a contractor with whom he has business, had gone to a bathhouse or gymnasium at three o'clock in the afternoon, but in Stockholm it is a common reply to an inquiry. During winter afternoons you can usually find anybody you want by going to his favorite gymnasium or bathhouse, just as you would look for him at his club in Chicago.

There is a distinctive dress for the exercise. The patrons take off their street clothing and put on light woolen shirts and trousers, and canvas shoes on their bare feet, and, standing in rows, go through a series of motions under the command of their instructor to exercise the arms, legs, neck, and every other part of the body, gently, not violently. The idea is movement, not exertion, and the muscles are restrained. The arm is raised slowly with self-resistance. No clubs or dumb-bells are used, only a gentle motion like the exercise of the children in the schools. After twenty minutes or half an hour of this the class marches in a column, still going through the same movements; then they run, following their leader, doing everything that he does, until at the end of an hour the body is in a glow, the blood is pulsating in every vein, the perspiration is oozing from every pore, every muscle is limbered up and strengthened, and every nerve tingles. There is regular gymnasium apparatus for those who like more violent exercise. Then a bath is taken, followed by a cold plunge and violent rubbing with massage, after which a man is in shape to go home to his dinner with a good appetite.

In October every year the Scandinavian Gymnastic Instructors' Association meets in Stockholm for several weeks, at which lectures are delivered, papers are read, and discussions are held upon all branches of their work. These meetings are quite as important as annual conventions of the bar or medical associations, and are not only attended by gymnastic instructors, but by physicians generally, for every Swedish physician must be well versed in medical gymnastics, particularly in what is known as *kinesitherapym* or movement cure, which embraces active, passive, and resisting movements, as well as massage, for the latter is the basis of medical gymnastics.

The Swedes have accepted this treatment as a specific for nearly all diseases, deformities, and weaknesses of the body; for internal complaints, for the lungs, the heart, and the digestive organs. It removes superfluous tissue, and this is the reason you see so few fat men in Sweden, notwithstanding their beer-drinking propensities, and why the women keep their youthful shape until old age.

It is a spectacle to witness in some of the gymnastic institutes venerable and dignified gentlemen going through comical motions and assuming ridiculous postures with great activity and zeal, keeping time to the music of a band in the adjoining café.

In Sweden doctors never send bills to their patients, but trust entirely to their generosity. Each family has an attending physician, who expects them to pay him by the year for his services, according to their wealth and the amount of attention they receive. Ten dollars a year in our money is a good fee; one hundred dollars is princely. At the beginning of the year you put the amount in an envelope and send it to the doctor by a messenger with your card. He sends back his card with an acknowledgment of thanks and the compliments of the season. It is very bad form to talk about it, although grateful patients often write their physicians affectionate letters of gratitude for his devotion and the benefit he has brought them. It is a good deal like the relation between a minister and his parishioners in other countries, and the annual contribution for the support of the doctor is just as voluntary as the contribution to the treasury of the church. If there is any reason why one should feel grateful to the doctors; if you or your children have suffered a severe illness and he has pulled you through, he expects a present in addition to the annual honorarium, just as you would send the minister a present after a marriage or a funeral or some other special occasion at which his services are required. The amount you pay depends upon your ability and the value of his services, but it is a violation of the most sacred canon of professional etiquette for a doctor to ask compensation or question the amount he receives. He keeps no accounts of his visits and no books. If a stranger or an acquaintance who does not contribute regularly makes one call or two upon the doctor to ask his advice or a prescription, he leaves something on the table, but it would be equivalent to an insult if he should ask for a bill.

When a person is very sick, he is taken to a hospital. Sweden has some of the best hospitals in the world. His own doctor looks after him there, assisted by the house physician and nurses, who expect fees, but the regular doctor gets none. He supervises the treatment and acts as adviser to the house physician.

The government pays subsidies to doctors in remote parts of the country, just as it pays the salaries of the ministers where the people are so poor that they can not support a doctor and a parson. In fact, all the clergymen of the established church are paid by the government and are government officials. The members of their parishes give them presents, something on the donation party order, because their salaries are small, and if there happen to be rich men in the parish, it is their custom to send around a handsome present to the minister's wife or to himself on Christmas Day.

The Swedes have a short summer, and so far as possible spend it in the open air. Every citizen of Stockholm who can afford it has a place in the country, no matter how humble or primitive it may be, and if he can not afford a cabin, he pitches a tent in the woods under the pine trees, and if necessary cooks his own meals. The banks of the lakes and rivers throughout the entire kingdom—and there are more than 1,400 lakes in Sweden and 1,700 islands in the Stockholm Skärgard—are surrounded by such dwellings and camps, for the Swedes love the water. Those who are compelled to remain in town take their meals and spend their evenings at the open-air cafes, which are found in every part of the city with bands of music, and take daily excursions on the boats which ply through the fjord and the lakes which encircle the town. In the suburbs are circuses, open-air theaters, concert gardens, and other forms of entertainments, simple and serious. A number of fine restaurants are maintained in the parks, where people can get a good dinner and spend the evening under the cool foliage, listening to an orchestral concert or a band. Every form of outdoor amusement is furnished, and the people eat, drink, and are merry, making the most of their time from June to September before the long and dreary winter comes upon them.

The working classes have their simple amusements also, and during the summer evenings in every village there is music and dancing, even if an accordion or jewsharp is the only instrument to be obtained. The national dances are quite energetic, and furnish a form of exercise which lazy people would not admire, but both the men and women of Sweden are famous for their muscular strength, and the young woman who can dance down her companions is as much of a hero as the champion wrestler of the town. Those who can not enjoy the opportunity of visiting rural Sweden will find in the suburbs of Stockholm, at the favorite resort and place of amusement of the common people, a perfect representation of Swedish country life. It is called Skansen, and is rural Sweden in miniature. It is a patriotic and scientific enterprise, conceived and undertaken by the late Dr. Artur Hazelius, an eminent ethnologist, for the purpose of preserving the habits and customs of the Scandinavian races. In no country of Europe, excepting perhaps Russia and Turkey, have the people adhered to the manner and costumes of their fathers so tenaciously as in Sweden, and the life of past generations is preserved in its picturesqueness. The conservatism of the people, their tenacious preference for their own ways and means has kept out innovations, and very few changes have been made since the beginning of the eighteenth century. But fearing that the peasants of Sweden, like all other peoples, would sooner or later surrender to modern fashions, Dr. Hazelius attempted to collect at Skansen actual types representing every industry, activity, and national trait. His thought was expressed in a motto inscribed over one of the gates of this outdoor museum:

"The day will come when all our gold will not be sufficient to buy an accurate picture of the times long past."

He procured from the king a rocky plateau on the edge of a royal park known as *Djurgarden*, covered with crippled pines and resembling the wild, uncultivated, neglected landscape in Dalecaria or Norrland, the two most interesting portions of Sweden. By careful landscape gardening, without destroying its natural beauty, he introduced broad paths, restaurants, cafes, band stands, and other places for the merry to meet and hold their festivals, and for the students to sing their songs, and he reserved a part of the grounds in its natural condition, where the lovers of nature can find a quiet retreat among the gloom of a pine grove. It has become the most popular resort in Sweden, particularly in the long summer evenings, and when a man can not reach the country, Skansen is never too far. It is accessible by street-cars and by boats, and is not more than half an hour's walk from the palace.

Here the "folk festivals," for which the Swedish poets have composed their most beautiful songs, are held every spring; here the national holidays are celebrated as in olden times, both in summer and winter, and national customs are preserved with great care and amid surroundings that give them a realistic tone, like the true thing. Dr. Hazelius secured original types of peasant houses from every part of the country where they have individual or unique character. From the huts of the fishermen on the south coast of the Scandinavian peninsula to the camps of the Lapps in the frozen zone, every feature of Swedish country life is represented. The Lapps brought their dogs and reindeer, and live exactly as they do upon the snowy plains of the polar regions.

With the forty acres that compose the park are about one hundred and twenty-five people, living exactly as their forefathers lived and practicing the primitive customs that prevailed two centuries ago in the agricultural districts of the kingdom. They wear the same costumes, eat the same kind of food, use the same kind of dishes, and preserve so far as possible every feature of their daily life. Every one of the provinces of Sweden which has a distinctive dress or unique custom is represented by the actual people who have always lived that way. Every man and woman continues their former occupations. There is no theatrical business about it, no imitations on the grounds; everything is genuine.

Three or four times a week at sunset, after their daily work is done, the peasants gather for a dance at a central place, which is always surrounded by a large crowd of spectators, and is the greatest attraction of Skansen. On alternate nights the dancing is by the children, of whom there are thirty-seven under fifteen years of age living in the cabins with their parents, dressed just like their great-great-grandfathers and grand mothers when they were of the same age. The music for the dancing is furnished by old-fashioned instruments, and none but old-fashioned tunes are allowed. There is a society in Sweden known as *Svenska Folkdansens Vänner* for preserving the Swedish national peasant dances and for encouraging their use in the higher circles of society in preference to the French dances.

There are several fine museums and picture galleries in Sweden. The national gallery in Stockholm, which is across the bay from the royal palace, and the Northern Museum founded in 1872 by Dr. Hazelius. Then there is the Royal Opera and the National Theater, so that the people of Stockholm do not want for places of amusement in winter as well as summer.

The father of athletic sports in Sweden is Lieutenant Colonel Victor Gustaf Balck, who holds a military position in the garrison at Stockholm. He introduced lawn tennis, cricket, baseball and football, and has established numerous athletic clubs in different parts of the country. Sailing is popular, there being many yacht clubs with good houses and fleets. And swimming is a part of the national education, nearly every man, woman, and child in Sweden taking naturally to the water and being able to swim. Everybody can skate as well as swim. In the cities rinks can be found with music and many conveniences. In Stockholm there is a general skating club, with a rink large enough to accommodate six thousand skaters, and popular fêtes given there at intervals during the winter are attended by the royal family and members of the court, and are regarded as important social functions. All skating is done upon the numerous lakes, and often during the long nights of the winter hundreds of people, young and old, will gather at an early hour—it gets dark at four o'clock in the afternoon—and spend the entire night skating by moonlight. A big fire is built in some convenient place for the crowd, and smaller fires by individual parties, who bring luncheon with them and have a picnic in the snow in the winter. In various parts of the country, national and international skating contests are held, and winners in local tournaments, both for speed and fancy skating, are sent to Stockholm to contest for the grand prizes against the crack skaters of Norway, Denmark, Russia, and northern Germany.

But the national winter sport of all Scandinavia is skeeing—skimming over the snow on snow-shoes. There is no more vigorous or exciting exercise. In the country districts men and women alike are educated to the use of snowshoes from childhood. As soon as boys and girls are old enough to skate, they put on skees of a size appropriate to their stature, and are quite as agile and daring as their elders. It requires nerve, skill, and muscular strength to skee, and a person who has never tried snow-shoes always finds it difficult to use them. It is a sport to which people must be trained from childhood. A skilful "skeer" can make a mile in two minutes.

Ice yachting and sailing on skates are two of the oldest and most popular national sports, and are practiced in both Sweden and Norway by all classes. All the ice yachts and snow-shoes are home-made, and in the country districts many of the skates.[p]

CHAPTER XVII
THE NEWSPAPERS OF NORWAY AND SWEDEN

There are seven hundred and fifty-one newspapers and periodicals in Sweden, including fifty-two dailies. Stockholm has twelve dailies, seven published in the morning and five in the evening, which is a large number for a city of three hundred and ten thousand inhabitants, and the wonder is how they all manage to exist. None of them is as large as the ordinary dailies in the United States. It is the practice of the Swedish editors to waste very little room in headlines, and to condense as much as possible. They state facts without padding or comment, and manage to bring the daily allowance of news within ten or twelve columns. There is usually a continued story, three or four articles of a literary character, a couple of columns of clippings and miscellany, and the same amount of editorial. The balance of the paper is given up to advertising, but with all that it is seldom necessary to print more than four pages. The morning papers stick to the blanket sheet.

Most of the Stockholm papers have a good advertising patronage, which runs to display at times. The Swedish business men have learned that it pays to advertise. The rates are much lower than in the United States. The ordinary want ad. costs from seven to ten cents, and for display advertisements the rates run from two and one-half to twenty cents a line, according to the location. In the semi-weekly edition of *Aftonbladet*, which is considered the best advertising medium in Sweden on account of its large circulation and superior class of readers, display ads. in preferred places cost about twenty-eight cents a line.

The subscription price corresponds. You can have any one of the evening papers delivered at your house for $3 a year, and the highest rate for the morning dailies is $5 a year. It is worth while to know that postmasters in Sweden will receive subscriptions for newspapers published in any part of the world. A small fee is exacted to cover the amount of postage and the stationery required in forwarding the subscription.

The father of cheap newspapers in Sweden is Anders Jeurling, the publisher of *Stockholm-Tidningen* and *Hyvad Nytt i Dag*, who started the first-named journal about twelve years ago and sold it on the street for two *öre*, which is about one-half cent. Now the price of the former is four *öre*, about one cent, and of the latter a half cent. The former paper has the largest circulation in the city of Stockholm, its ordinary edition reaching about one hundred thousand copies, but *Aftonbladet* exceeds it in the country. Mr. Jeurling has the reputation of being the ablest publisher in Sweden, and is a better business man than the editor. He has made a fortune out of his papers on the theory that the people care more for news than for politics. Mr. Adolph Hallgren is the editor-in-chief of *Stockholms-Tidningen*, and the managing editor is Mr. F. Zethraens, who studied journalism in the office of the Chicago *Record-Herald*.

The official paper of the Swedish government is *Post och Inriches Tidning*, which was founded as far back as 1645, and is one of the oldest periodicals in the world. For more than a century it has been published under the auspices of the Swedish Academy, an organization of eighteen of the most learned scholars and philosophers in the kingdom. The editor is Dr. J.A. Spilhammar, a very learned gentleman, who, on account of his position, is naturally conservative and discreet in all his utterances.

Aftonbladet, a liberal evening paper, to which I have already alluded, has the greatest circulation in Sweden, the daily edition varying from one hundred and fifty thousand to one hundred and sixty thousand copies, and it is one of the most influential forces in the kingdom. The editor, Harald Sohlman, is regarded is an able writer and shrewd business man. He is also editor and publisher of *Dagen*, a morning paper, liberal in politics, which has a circulation of about forty thousand copies, and is sold at three *öre*—about three-quarters of a cent. *Aftonbladet's* semi-weekly edition goes into every corner of the kingdom, has a high literary standard, contains correspondence from all the European capitals, and has a special department devoted to news concerning the Swedes and Swedish affairs in America.

The most conservative of all Swedish papers is *Nya Dagligt Allehanda*, edited by Dr. J.A. Bjorklund. Its circulation is confined almost exclusively to the nobility and wealthier classes, and is said to be more loyal to the government than royalty itself.

Vart Land, another conservative paper, edited by Professor Gustaf Torelius, an eminent author and scholar, is an organ of the Swedish state church, and on that account is taken by every Lutheran clergyman and active layman in the kingdom. It contains the official announcement of the minister of religion and the archbishop, and is especially given to news of an ecclesiastical character. Its most prominent writer is Dr. C.D. af Wirsén, one of "the immortal eighteen" of the Swedish Academy and a lyric poet of reputation.

Svenska Morgonbladet, another religious daily, opposes *Vart Land*, and represents the dissenters from the established church. Its circulation, according to its sarcastic competitors, "is limited to those who have been saved." Its most eminent contributor and patron is Dr. Peter Paul Waldenström, founder and leader of the Free Lutheran Church, "the Swedish Moody." Scarcely a week passes without an article from his pen in *Morgonbladet*, which gives that paper its standing among Free Lutherans.

Dagbladet is the only paper in Stockholm which is issued twice a day, and it has also a Sunday edition. It styles itself in politics a "moderate," but is more popular among the conservatives than the liberals. Having the city printing, it is not inclined to quarrel with its bread and butter.

Dagens Nyheter, a liberal morning paper, made a fortune for Rudolph Wall, its founder, who died a millionaire. It is considered one of the most profitable newspaper properties in Europe. It sells for a cent and a quarter, and has a circulation of about thirty thousand.

The Stockholm paper which imitates the American press most closely is *Svenska Dagbladet*, ably edited by Helmer Key, a doctor of philosophy, and C.G. Tengwall, who is regarded as one of the best all-around newspaper men in Sweden. It has the best class of contributors of any of the Swedish papers in a literary way, including Professor Oscar Levertin, Verner von Heidenstam, the poet, Tor Hedberg, an art and literary critic, and Ellen Key, the authoress, and the most influential woman in Sweden. The paper has a large circulation among the thinking people of the country, and exercises a wide influence.

The official organ of the Royal Yacht Club, the Royal Jockey Club, and all representative Swedish sport clubs, is the *Ny Tidning för Idrott*, which is owned by Count Clarence von Rosen, one of the grandsons of the late Mrs. Bloomfield Moore, of Philadelphia. The count, himself the finest rider in the Swedish army, edits the horse news, while Colonel Victor Balck, the father of modern Swedish sports, and Alex. Lindman are the editors. *Ny Tidning för Idrott* has a regular correspondent in America. Hjalmar Branting, leader of the socialists in Sweden and a member of the second chamber of parliament, is editor of *Social Demokraten*, the organ of his party. Although a man of aristocratic origin, he has cast his lot with the laboring classes. He is a man of great force of character, an able writer, an eloquent speaker, and is generally respected even by those who can not approve his views. The circulation of his paper is almost exclusively confined to the laboring classes.

The compensation of newspaper men in Sweden is much less than in the United States. The highest salary paid to an editor-in-chief is $4,000, while the lowest for that position is about $1,500. Managing editors are paid from $1,200 to $2,000 a year, and ordinary reporters from $300 to $750 a year. Contributors of fame receive special rates. The price for news items is two and one-half cents a line. Space writers seem to be paid more in proportion than the regular members of the staff, but the difference is more apparent than real, because of the tendency to condensation. Articles in the Swedish papers are seldom more than half a column long.

Stockholm has several comic papers, even more in proportion to population than we have in the United States. The most prominent are *Strix, Puck, Söndags-Nisse, Kasper* and *Nya Nisse*. They are small and comparatively insignificant, and sell for two and one-half cents a copy. They satirize politicians with good humor, and their cartoons are based upon current events. There are several literary weeklies, monthlies, and other periodicals, for Swedes are great readers and, unlike the Americans, have not lost their taste for poetry. A poet enjoys a much higher position and larger income from his writings in Sweden than at home.

There is a Press Club in Stockholm with four hundred and forty members, of whom twenty-two are women. In 1901 the club arranged "a week of festivals," including military tournaments, public entertainments and a fair, and closed with a masquerade ball at the Royal Opera House to raise funds for a building. It was a great success. King Oscar accepted an invitation, and enjoyed himself very much among his "colleagues," as he called them. The king was always considerate to newspaper men. He appreciated the purpose and understood the requirements of reporters, and never failed to assist them whenever he was able to do so. Hence he was very popular among them, and they reciprocated by showing their appreciation in every possible way. The old king once said to Hjalmar Branting, the socialist editor:

"We have different opinions, Branting, but we are both working for the welfare of our country."

In 1897, during the international congress of the press at Stockholm, the king gave the editors a banquet at the Royal Castle at Drottningholm, and mingled among them as "one of yourselves." He also proposed a toast in most complimentary language.

Oscar II made many speeches, and upon occasions of great formality he used manuscript, but generally spoke without notes, preparing himself in advance by study and reflection. When he spoke from manuscript, he invariably furnished copies to the press, and was never known to request that part of his speech be suppressed.

Reporters are invariably admitted to state ceremonials. There is very little secrecy about the Stockholm court, and intrigue is entirely unknown in Swedish politics. There are no mysteries in the council chamber and no skeletons in the royal closet. Hence the doors are open, and the reporters can come and go as they please. As a natural consequence comparatively little attention is paid to affairs at the palace. There is an announcement every morning of the movements of the king and the royal family and occurrences of public interest, but with very little detail, and the newspapers depend upon the officials to furnish the information voluntarily. Reporters are seldom sent to the palace unless some special inquiry is necessary.

The story is told that once when Oscar II went to Gothenburg to attend a dedication or opening of something or other, where he was expected to make a speech, he was intercepted at the railway station by an enterprising reporter who wanted a copy of his speech. The paper was to be published that afternoon, and there would be no time for a stenographer to write out his notes afterward. The king greeted him pleasantly and explained that he had no manuscript; that he intended to speak without notes. The reporter was very much dissappointed, and confided to the king that he was a new man and that his future standing with his employer might be seriously affected if he failed to get the speech. King Oscar responded sympathetically, invited the reporter to get into his carriage, and while they were driving to the hotel, gave a brief synopsis of what he expected to say.

Newspapers in Norway are not so good an investment; in fact, none of them may be considered financial ventures. As a rule, they have to be assisted by the government or by political clubs in order to survive. Their subscription lists are limited, the largest circulation in Norway not exceeding fifteen thousand and few publications print more than five thousand copies, while advertising pays not more than ten or twelve cents a line at top prices in the most expensive papers.

An ordinary newspaper reporter in Norway receives a salary of about $5 a week, while the most competent editors are satisfied with $20 or $25. Norway was the last of the European countries, except Turkey, to adopt the art of printing, notwithstanding its early famous literature, but to-day has four hundred and twenty-nine newspapers and periodicals, an average of one to every five thousand of the population; one hundred and ninety-six are political newspapers; eighty-eight are literary weeklies, and one hundred and forty-five are reviews, magazines, professional, religious, and scientific publications.

Norske Intelligens-Seddeler is one of the oldest papers in the world, having been founded in Christiania in 1763, and has been the organ of the government from the beginning. For a century and a quarter its contents were limited to advertisements and official announcements. It was a sort of a government gazette, but when Hjalmar Loken took hold of it, ten or twelve years ago, he changed its character entirely and has turned it into a good modern newspaper and a vigorous advocate of government measures, exercising a wide influence through its columns.

Monopolies were formerly granted to newspapers in Norway. The government allowed only one paper to be published within the limits of an ecclesiastical diocese, or at least only the favored paper was permitted to receive money for the publication of advertisements. Competitors resorted to all sorts of ingenious methods, by issuing pamphlets and 'handbills and such things, that a free discussion of political issues might be had, but it was not until 1786 that the last monopoly, which happened to be in the city of Trondhjem, expired. In 1814 freedom of the press was granted by the new constitution, and from that date the political agitators have found expression in various publications, and partisanship has often risen to a bitterness that would not be permitted in other countries. The Norway newspapers have not known a censor since that date.

Morganbladet, the first daily, was established in 1819, and has played an important part in the political affairs of the. country. It is still very influential, being edited with great ability by Mr. Nils Vogt. Björnson, the author, has been connected with two newspapers—the first, *Krydseren*, a literary weekly which survived only a few years, and *Verdens Gang*, which has been published since 1868 as the leading organ of the liberal party. Among its editors and contributors have been other distinguished men, poets, dramatists, and novelists. Nearly every writer of distinction has contributed to its columns, for most of the thinking men of Norway are liberals. Since 1878 Mr. Thommessen has been the editor, and he was the first to modernize the Norwegian press by printing cable dispatches, cartoons, caricatures and other illustrations.

Dagbladet is also a widely read and influential daily, under the editorship of Mr. A.T. Omholt, and has a large circulation. Its list of contributors has included some of the most distinguished writers of the country. There are numerous other dailies of more or less influence and circulation, and all the trades and occupations have organs, as in the United States. In every town and almost every village, a weekly or semi-weekly is published, usually by the liberal party, and sometimes by other parties. Even Hammerfest, the most northerly town in the world, which lies in the Arctic Circle, has two enterprising weeklies.[q]

CHAPTER XVIII
NORWEGIAN FOLK SONGS

If the dwellers of the deep fjords, the somber fir-clad mountain valleys, and the bleak ice-fields do not "open their lips so readily for song" as the people of southern lands where the sun creates an eternal spring, it is not because they are without lyric power, as is clearly apparent from the rich and varied folk-songs and the splendid creative work of Edvard Grieg.

The Norwegian folk-songs, spring dances, hallings, and wedding marches, have been well characterized as the outpourings of the inner lives of the common people, the expression of their dauntless energy, their struggles and aspirations. The folk-song of Norway, more than in any other land, embodies the character and expresses the tendencies of Viking life, ancient and modern. It bears the unmistakable marks of weal and woe of Norse life, the strongly marked and regularly introduced rythms of the developed and developing national character. And while an undercurrent of melancholy runs through most of it, it is, after all, the faithful interpreter of the lives of isolated and solitary occupants of fjords, fjelds, and dalen.

The folk-songs of Norway are singularly typical of the country and its inhabitants. Some "seem to take us into the dense forest among mocking echoes from, the life outside; others show us the trolls tobogganing down the highest peaks of Norway; in some we feel human souls hovering over reefs; in others, memories of the old sun-lit land flit before us; but in none do we meet with sentimentalism, despondency, or disconsolateness." But with their weird and minor strains, and their odd jumps from low tones to high, on first acquaintance they strike the hearer as strange and elusive.

Some of the epic songs, as Telemarken, are of great antiquity. But it was not until the last century that Norse tone artists discovered the wealth that had long been cherished by the peasants of the fjords and mountain valleys. Lindeman (1812-1887) was the first to recognize the musical significance of Norwegian folk-songs. He collected many hundred national ballads, hymns and dances, and called attention to their richness and variety as thematic material for a school of national music. In Lindeman's collection will be found songs which tell of the heroic exploits of old Norse vikings, kings, and earls of the heathen days of Thor and Odin, together with lyrics, deep and ardent, which sing of the loves, the joys, and the sorrows of the humbler Christian folks.

The Hardanger violin, the lur and the langeleik have played a leading role in the development of Norwegian folk-songs and dances. The Hardanger instrument is more arched than the ordinary violin; there are four strings over the finger-board and four underneath, the latter of fine steel wire, acting as sympathetic strings. The men of the Hardanger fjord have long been distinguished for the workmanship and tonal qualities of their violins, and with them the peasants have improvised the rich and varied impressions of nature which we find embodied in folk-songs. The lur is a long wooden instrument, of the trumpet order, and is usually made of birch bark. It is much used in the mountains. The langeleik, or Norwegian harp, is a long, narrow, box-like stringed instrument, something of the character of the ancient zither. It has seven strings and sound holes, but its tone is weak and monotonous.

The national dances of Norway have bold rythms which at once arrest the attention. Perhaps the most characteristic is the hailing, a solo dance in two-four time. It is usually danced by young men in country barns, and its most striking feature is the kicking of the beam of the ceiling. In the story of Nils the fiddler, in his novel *Arne*, Björnson has given this account of the hailing: "The music struck up, a deep silence followed, and he began. He dashed forward along the floor, his body inclining to one side, half aslant, keeping time to the fiddle. Crouching down, he balanced himself, now on one foot, now on the other, flung his legs crosswise under him, sprang up again, and then moved on aslant as before. The fiddle was handled by skilful fingers, and more and more fire was thrown into the tune. Nils threw his head back and suddenly his boot heel touched the beam."

The spring dance is less vigorous, but more graceful than the hailing. It is a round dance in three-quarter time, in which two persons, or groups of two, participate. It is danced with a light, springing step, and has been compared with the mazurka by Liszt. Like the hailing, however, it is markedly individual in its pleasing combinations of tones. Forestier says of the spring dance of Norway: "There is a freshness, a sparkle, and energy, a graceful life about it that is invigorating."

If Lindeman was the first to collect folk-songs and dances in Norway, Ole Bull (1810-1880) was the first to popularize them. He was, as Grieg once declared, a pathbreaker for the young national music. At the early age of nineteen he sallied forth with his fiddle and wherever he appeared in Europe and America he played the folk-music and national dances of

Norway. The favor which he found encouraged his countrymen. His brilliant career glorified musical Norway; gave it confidence to assert itself, and serve as the inspiration of a long list of creative tone artists—Kjerulf, Nordraak, Grieg, Svendsen, Winter-Hjelm, Sindling, and Behrens—to write out and arrange for voice and modern instruments the music that had so long been preserved in the memories of the people.

The best art-made music of Norway has been built upon the folk-songs and dances of the common people. Halfdan Kjerulf (1815-1868) was the first serious composer of the new art school. He lived during the trying period of Norwegian storm and stress, but he wrote something like a hundred compositions, and in his songs is found "the bud of national feeling which has burst into full bloom in Grieg."

Richard Nordraak (1842-1866), during his brief career, set to music several of Björnson's plays, and composed some strong pianoforte pieces and songs. "He was," says Siewers, "a man with a bold fresh way of looking at things, strong artistic interests, an untiring love of work, and deep national feeling. He had decided influence upon his friend Grieg's artistic views, and he is the connecting link between Kjerulf and Grieg in the chain of Norwegian musical art."

Otto Winter-Hjelm, who, with Grieg, attempted to establish a conservatory of music at Christiania after their return from Germany in the sixties, contributed much to the national art of Norway by his excellent arrangements of hallings and spring dances for piano and violin. Thomas Thellefsen (1823-1874), a pupil and friend of Chopin, was distinguished as a national composer as well as a pianist, and Carl F.E. Neupert (1842-1888), who lived in America six years, did much by his concert tours and teaching to dignify Norse music.

Johan Severin Svendsen, while a Norwegian by birth and training, has expatriated himself by his long residence in Denmark. So far as his compositions have national flavor they are German. Johan Selmer, while a prolific composer, will probably be best remembered as a conductor. Christian Sinding, after Grieg, is the best-known Norwegian composer. His productions range from symphonies and symphonic poems through chamber music to romances. He is credited with a wide range of musical ideas, deep artistic earnestness, and bold power of expression; but his compositions in the larger forms are thought unduly noisy and restless.

Two women who have helped to make the music history of Norway are Agatha Backer-Gröndahl and Catharinus Elling. Mrs. Backer-Gröndahl was a pupil, first of Kjerulf and Winter-Hjelm, and later of Kullak, Hans von Bülow, and Liszt. Many of her songs and instrumental pieces display fine artistic feeling and musical scholarship of no mean order. Catharinus Elling has ventured into the larger fields of music-forms, and has produced operas, symphonies, and oratorios, as well as chamber music and songs. Her music drama, "The Cossacks," is her most ambitious work.

Says Henry T. Finck, an able American music critic: "When I had revelled in the music of Chopin and Wagner, Liszt and Franz, to the point of intoxication, I fancied that the last word had been said in harmony and melody; when lo! I came across the songs and piano pieces of Grieg, and once more found myself moved to tears of delight." Edvard Grieg (1843-1907) undoubtedly occupies the foremost place among Norwegian composers. He is the highest representative of the Norse element in music, "the great beating heart of Norwegian musical art."

Grieg's *genere* pieces represent the pearls of his compositions. The arrangements of folk-songs and dances for the piano in "Pictures of Popular Life" (opus 19) are characterized by consummate lyric skill; and Ole Bull once declared that they were the finest representations of Norse life that had been attempted. Grieg wrote one hundred and twenty-five songs, most of which take high rank. Finck is of the opinion that fewer fall below par than in the list of any other song writer. He adds: "I myself believe that Grieg in some of his songs equals Schubert at his best; indeed, I think he should and will be ranked ultimately as second to Schubert only; but it is in his later works that he rises to such heights, not in the earliest ones, in which he was still a little afraid to rely on his wings."

When it is recalled that Grieg was a pianist of exceptional merit, the large place occupied by pianoforte pieces—twenty-eight of the seventy-three opus numbers—it is easily understood. Grieg's piano pieces are brief, but they are veritable gems. The Jumbo idea in music still lingers with minor professionals. They shrug their shoulders, remarks Finck, and exclaim: "Yes, that humming bird *is* very beautiful, but of course it can not be ranked as high as an ostrich. Don't you see how small it is?"

Grieg composed nine works for the orchestra; and here, as in lyric art-songs and pianoforte pieces, he reveals himself as a consummate master in painting delicate yet glowing colors. The music which he set to Ibsen's *Peer Gynt* brought him the largest measure of fame as an orchestral composer. Indeed it was more cordially received than the drama, as is indicated by this criticism by Hanslick: "Perhaps in a few years Ibsen's *Peer Gynt* will live only through Grieg's music, which, to my taste, has more poetry and artistic intelligence in every number than the whole five-act monstrosity of Ibsen." Among other notable orchestral and chamber music numbers may be mentioned a setting of Björnson's *Sigurd the Crusader, Bergliot*, based upon the sagas of the Norse kings, a suite composed for the two hundredth anniversary of Ludwig Holberg, and a number of choice chamber music pieces.

It may be remarked that Edvard Grieg has not only given Norway a conspicuous place on the map of musical Europe, but that he has influenced unmistakably composers of the rank of Tschaikowsky, the Russian; Paderewski, the Pole; Eugene d'Albert, the Scotch-English-German; Richard Strauss, the German; and our own lamented Edward McDowell, the American. "From every point of view that interests the music lover," says Mr. Finck, "Grieg is one of the most original geniuses in the musical world of the present or past. His songs are a mine of melody, surpassed in wealth only by Schubert's, and that only because there are more of Schubert's. In originality of harmony and modulation he has only six equals: Bach, Schubert, Chopin, Schumann, Wagner, and Liszt. In rythmic invention and combination he is inexhaustible, and as orchestrator he ranks among the most fascinating. To speak of such a man—seven-eighths of whose works are still music of the future—as a writer of 'dialect,' is surely the acme of unintelligence. If Grieg did stick to the fjord and never got out of it, even his German critics ought to thank heaven for it. Grieg in a fjord is much more picturesque and more interesting to the world than he would have been in the Elbe or the Spree."

While Norway has neither permanent opera nor permanent orchestras, she has produced concert virtuosi of a high order. Ole Bull, the so-called violin-king, already referred to, was unsurpassed in his day. Among piano artists may be named the talented composer, Mrs. Agatha Backer-Gröndahl, Thomas Thellefsen, Edmund Neupert, Martin Knutzen, and the great composer Edvard Grieg. The flutist Olaf Svenssen and the vocal artists Thorvald Lammers, Ingeborg Oselio-Björnson, and Ellen Gulbranson, have also brought distinction to their country.

The male choirs of Norway have always played a leading rôle in the music life of the nation. The students', merchants', and artists' singing clubs at Christiania during the past seventy-five years, have had artistic as well as patriotic aims. Festivals, after the pattern of those held at Cincinnati, and Worcester and Springfield, Massachusetts, have also contributed toward the development of national music. The most eminent choral leaders in Norway have been Johan D. Behrens, F.A. Reissinger, and O.A. Gröndahl.

The Norwegian Musical Union has also been active in the development of tonal ideals. Its aim has been to provide chamber concerts of a high order. Grieg and Svendsen were its first conductors. They were succeded by Ole Olsen, who combined the talents of orchestral leader with those of composer, chorister, and band leader. For many years he directed the Second Brigade Band at Christiania with the rank of captain. Johan Selmer, also a composer, succeeded Olsen in the direction of the Musical Union; and Iver Holier, a composer of symphonies, orchestral suites, chamber music, and vocal scores, followed Selmer. Other orchestral leaders are Johan Hennum, Per Winge, and Johan Halvorsen,

CHAPTER XIX
THE WOMEN OF NORWAY AND SWEDEN

No volume dealing with Scandinavian life would be complete without some tribute to the women of Norway and Sweden. They are magnificent specimens wherever you may find them—in the kitchen, the factory, the harvest field, the hospital, the schoolhouse, the drawing-room, or the palace. They are good mothers, good daughters, and good wives, and while their devotion to their sons, husbands, and fathers is not surpassed by their sisters in any land, they are at the same time independent, self-reliant, and progressive to a degree that offers a striking contrast to the statue of the representatives of their sex in other countries of Europe. They give their best talents, affections, and strength; they ask the same in return. There is no country, not even the United States, where women exercise a wider influence, both direct and indirect in the home, the school, the church, upon the platform, and in the press. There is no other country in which the professions, trades, and other occupations are so free to them, or in which their opportunities are utilized with greater zeal, ability, and success. They work side by side with men upon the farms, in the factories, in mercantile establishments, counting-houses, government offices, and in art, science, and literature, and are equally capable, although, as in other lands, their pay for the same labor and equal results is less.

From the time that Margit Larsson saved Gustavus Vasa from capture by the Danish soldiers by hiding him in her cellar, the women of Sweden have exercised a powerful influence in politics, although it has been indirect, and the ablest and most progressive to-day prefer that their present political condition shall remain unchanged. They do not think it wise to extend the franchise any farther for fear that universal suffrage will result in the corruption of national politics, which is now comparatively pure. They prefer the present restrictions, which give the ballot only to women who pay taxes, because it deprives ignorant and incompetent women of a voice in the government, and avoids the dangers that often attend the participation of the masses in elections. They prefer to direct their efforts to securing an increase in women's wages, so that they may receive the same compensation as men for the same work, and hope to accomplish practical results by educating public sentiment and bringing moral pressure upon the employing class.

Speaking on this subject, an eminent Swedish writer says: "In the energetic campaign for the betterment of the condition of women, the Swedes have taken the first place among European nations. If one seeks the cause of it, it is found in part in the fact that in Sweden, since the remotest time, women have enjoyed a respect greater than in most of the other countries, but without doubt it is also due to the superiority of the intellect, judgment, and wisdom of Swedish women, and in later years to the numerical excess of women in our population. This has made the means of existence to single women a practical problem. During the present generation a great change has worked itself out in this sense, that the field of activity for women has been greatly enlarged. The activity of women, who at other times found ample domain in the multitude of occupations in the domestic life, has become less important in that respect and has grown in importance in the labor and occupations that in other countries are left exclusively to men."

The advancement of women in Sweden was greatly encouraged and assisted by the quiet influence of the late Queen Sophia and her sister-in-law, the late Princess Eugenie, the sister of Oscar II. The queen, always an intelligent, progressive Christian woman, with a profound consciousness of the responsibility attached to her official rank and influence, was a women's woman, and was habitually engaged in promoting movements for the benefit of her sex, and with due respect to the proprieties of her position. She never lost an opportunity to assist and encourage all who were engaged in advancing the physical, moral, and social well-being of the women of Sweden and Norway.

The association of Swedish Women, which is a branch of the International Council of Women, was organized in 1896, and has over twelve thousand members, its object being to promote the welfare of the sex, to educate them on all questions concerning their legal and social rights, to enlarge their sphere of activity, and to assist those who are thrown upon their own resources to earn their living. The active, practical work is done by subordinate societies devoted to particular interests, as, for example, the Fredrika Bremer Association manages a sick relief fund for wage earners, assists students in the universities and technical schools, finds employment for those who need it, conducts schools for trained nurses, keeps a register of women who are capable of performing various duties, and is continually engaged in works of benevolence.

Another organization, known as the Swedish Woman's Association for the Defense of Their Country, is purely patriotic, and was organized in 1884 in connection with the movement for the increase of the army, for the purpose of educating public opinion. It has forty affiliated local committees carrying on a propaganda of patriotism. There is a women's club at Stockholm whose special purpose is to protect working women from persecution by their employers and others, to educate them concerning legal rights of women wage-earners, and to furnish legal advice and counsel to those who are in trouble. The seamstresses have an alliance, and the shop girls are organized into a union.

The advancement of women commenced under the leadership and inspiration of the late Fredrika Bremer, the famous authoress, who is well known in the United States because of her frequent visits here and her literary works. She was the pioneer of the movement to improve the condition of women morally, socially, and intellectually.

Sweden was the first country to recognize the property rights of women. This was due to an event that occurred a thousand years ago. While the king and his army were engaged in foreign wars, the Danes invaded the province of Smoland, when the women armed themselves to defend their homes. They were led to battle by the beautiful Blenda, who defeated the invaders and drove them from the country. In recognition of their heroism the king proclaimed a decree granting the women of the country property rights, and it has been since recognized as the law of the land.

All the professions and occupations common to men are open to the women of Sweden, and in 1862 suffrage was granted women in municipal affairs. They are permitted to vote at the election of delegates to conventions which choose members of the first chamber of parliament. These rights can now be exercised by all women who pay taxes. In Stockholm, however, a woman voter must be out of debt and the lawful owner of the property upon which the taxes are paid.

The members of the first chamber of the parliament, which corresponds to the United States Senate, are elected by conventions of delegates chosen at popular elections in the country and in cities by the members of the municipal councils. Therefore, as women have the right to vote for members of the municipal council and for delegates to these conventions, they participate indirectly in the election of the Swedish Senate; but comparatively few exercise the privilege.

Women of advanced views, aided by the members of the socialist party, are now seeking universal suffrage and a law making them eligible to parliament and to membership in the provincial and municipal councils. This proposition has not met with much favor, and the only time it has ever been brought to vote it was unanimously defeated in the first chamber of parliament and in the second by fifty-three nays to forty-four yeas, less than one-half the members present voting.

> The first woman to practice medicine in Sweden was Caroline Widerstrom, who is still living and occupies a prominent position in Stockholm. Her practice is as large and as profitable as that enjoyed by most of the men physicians.

The foremost woman in Sweden to-day in intellect and influence, in popular esteem and in public movements, and the recognized successor of Fredrika Bremer, is Ellen Key, an authoress and editorial writer upon *Svenska Dagbladet.*

In the system of local government in Norway, women now participate upon an equal basis with men. The movements which culminated May, 1901, had been going on since 1884 under the leadership of Miss Gina Krog, who may be called the Susan B. Anthony of Norway. In the latter year she organized a woman's suffrage association, delivered a series of lectures on the subject, and established a newspaper called the *Nyloende—* meaning "the new ground." Miss Krog is something over fifty years of age, of fine education and excellent family, and has been noted for her activity in literary and charitable affairs. She has been a teacher, a writer for the press, a director of charitable institutions, and has lived a life of great activity and usefulness, devoting her own means with generosity to the cause which she has undertaken.

The suffrage movement at first attracted little attention, but public sentiment grew slowly, and in 1890 Miss Krog succeeded in having a bill brought into the storthing giving women the right to vote in school matters. It received forty-four out of a total of one hundred and fourteen votes. The liberal party then made it an issue, and two years after the same bill received a majority in the storthing, but required two-thirds of the votes to pass. At that time a property qualification was required of men. The income tax returns were used as registration lists at the polls, and none but those who paid on incomes of $84 in the country and $92 in the city were allowed to vote.

The leaders of the movement for universal suffrage for men united forces with the women suffragists, and in 1898 accomplished their purpose. The women might have succeeded the same year but for an unfortunate division in their ranks. One faction wanted to limit suffrage to unmarried women who own property and deprive married women and dependent daughters and wage-earners of the ballot. But a compromise was finally arranged, the two factions were brought together, and in May, 1901, succeeded in accomplishing the purpose for which they have been engaged.

They received the support of a large portion of the conservative members of the storthing as well as the unanimous support of the liberal and radical parties, only twenty votes being cast in the negative.

The women of Norway do not propose to rest on their present success. Miss Krog is continuing the fight to secure the right of participation in national as well as municipal affairs, and believes that the women will have all the political rights of men in Norway within the next few years. She insists that public sentiment favors the cause and that parliament will take a step further soon and amend the law by making it broader and more general. Universities are open to women on an equal basis with men, and many women are taking advantage of the opportunity to secure the higher education, and if ever, like the women of Finland, they are allowed to sit in parliament, they will be amply fitted to do so.

Under the present law only women who pay a certain amount of taxes can vote. An unmarried woman living at home is deprived of the ballot unless she has an income of her own; a married woman can not vote unless either she or her husband has a stated income. Thus many of the most intelligent and progressive women of the country are still outside the suffrage line. Everybody in Norway who earns a dollar pays an income tax. It may be very small, but a certain percentage of each day's wages of every peasant goes into the government treasury. Every person in Norway declares that it is the least objectionable means of raising money for national and municipal expenses that has ever been tried there, and that it stimulates the patriotism of the people, who realize that they are contributors to the support of their government, and should take an active interest in its management.

Many of the wisest men in Norway consider the universal suffrage amendment to the constitution, which was passed in 1898, a mistake for this reason—because it removes a powerful incentive for men to accumulate money. The Norwegian has a large and natural fund of patriotism. He loves his country like the Swiss. Nowhere else do men and women have to work so hard for a living, but life is the more precious the harder one has to labor to sustain it. We value things according to their cost. In the tropics, where no man need work, human life is held cheaply. Men die and kill without compunction; they excite revolutions and overthrow governments, sparing neither themselves nor others. But in Norway, as in Switzerland, where it is a ceaseless struggle from the cradle to the grave, there is more national pride and patriotism than in any land, and the privilege of living and working and suffering is esteemed as the most precious inheritance of man.

Women in America who are working for the ballot have only to go to Norway to find that having a voice in the making of the laws of the country does not remove every obstacle to the progress of the sex; that there are still many injustices, and that the women work as hard as the men. The Norwegian woman usually carries a little more than her share of the load, and can support a husband without difficulty if he insists upon it. There is nothing so admirable in this world as a useful woman, particularly if she is married to a man inclined to leisure and loafing. In Norway and other countries of northern Europe the ballad, "I Love to See My Dear Old Mother Work," is something more than an affectionate sentiment. It has a practical significance, and is frequently found in husbands as well as sons.

Of all the labor that the women of Norway engage in, especially women in the rural districts, is the occupation of caring for the *saeter*. A *saeter* is a summer ranch or dairy farm peculiar, to Norway—a cabin among the pastures way up in the mountains, where the cattle are driven during the summer months and butter and cheese are made. Almost every large farmer has a *saeter*. When the spring field work at home has been finished, the cattle are taken thither by the young women and girls,—often twenty and sometimes forty miles away,—where they stay during the summer and make butter and cheese, gather hay, knit stockings, and embroider linen. The dwelling is usually a rude hut with a single room, mud floor, an open fireplace without chimney, and a few pieces of rough furniture. Sheds and pens surround the hut, and there are patches of enclosed ground where hay is made and where the younger members of the flock are protected. The cattle are called at night by a horn made of birch bark. When blown lustily, it gives a clear note not unlike the cornet, and the cattle invariably respond to its sound.

There is a good deal of romance about *saeter* life in books, but I should say that there is very little in actual experience. Many of the charming fairy stories in Norwegian literature have their scenes in those mountain dairies. The *saeter* girls (*saeterjenter* they are called), have a peculiar and melodious cattle call, known as the *Huldrelok*, which is said to have been inherited from the *Huldre-folk*, a species of fairy that are very pretty, but unfortunately have tails. Usually a young farmer falls in love with one of the girls, and when he discovers that she has a tail, is so shocked and disappointed that he throws himself over a precipice; or perhaps the *Huldre-folk* gobble him up and carry him off into the mountains of the *Josteldalsbrae* and keep him there, while the girl he left behind him grieves herself to death because of his desertion.

The dairy maids are supposed to have a peculiar costume, and photographs are often seen of them arrayed in picturesque dress, but I never saw them worn. In all the *saeters* I visited the clothes worn were very plain and ordinary, and seemed to have been selected for wear and not for looks.

We visited a *saeter* one day and found two young people in charge, a boy and a girl, neither of them over seventeen, we should judge from appearances. Their herd consisted of fifteen cows, and they expected to remain in that desolate country two or three months, making cheese and butter. Our little *saeterjenta* had the heart of a poet, although her brother seemed stupid, and even liberal presents of money did not wake him up or make him interesting. I do not suppose that this child had ever been twenty miles from the humble cabin in which she was born, but the wide, wide world had been opened to her through the books she had studied at school. She could talk a little English, and knew a good deal about the United States. She had a brother in Minnesota, and many of the boys and girls in the neighborhood had gone across the Atlantic and found homes on the saeterless prairies of our Northwest. She would like to go herself, she said, but her mother was old and feeble and the work of the farm fell upon her little shoulders. Yet she was brave and contented. Her mind was clear, her imagination active, and among her homely surroundings she had found food for thought and an opportunity to give expression to the poetic sentiments that inspired her. Each of her fifteen cows had a name. One she called Moon Lady, because she often wanders away at night; another the Crown Wearer, because of a peculiar tuft upon her head. She addressed them all in terms of affection and talked to them, seeking their sympathy, for, poor child, they and that stupid, tow-headed *broder* were her only companions.

In the little *saeterjenta* we have a type of the laboring peasant women of Norway and Sweden; all willingly industrious and all philosophically extracting some sweets out of the burdensome life they must live, and that is why I say they deserve a tribute, whether in the field or factory, the *saeter*, the common home, or the palace.[s]